Googlization of Libraries

This book includes a variety of articles which look critically and judiciously at Google and its products, with a focus on Google Scholar and Google Book Search. It also examines their usefulness in a public service context. Its ultimate aim is to assess the use of Google as a major information resource. Its subject matter deals with online megasearch engines and their influence on reference librarianship, the impact of Google on information seeking, librarianship and the development of book digitization projects in which Google Book Search plays its part.

This book will be of interest to librarians across all educational sectors, library science scholars and publishers.

This book was published as a special issue of the *Journal of Library Administration*.

William Miller is Dean of University Libraries at Florida Atlantic University. He formerly served as Head of Reference at Michigan State University, and as Associate Dean of Libraries at Bowling Green State University, Ohio. Presently, he teaches courses in English Literature and Library Science.

Rita M. Pellen is the Associate Director of Libraries at Florida Atlantic University. Previously, she was Assistant Director of Public Services and Head of the Reference Department.

Googlization of Libraries

Edited by William Miller and Rita M. Pellen

 Routledge
Taylor & Francis Group

LONDON AND NEW YORK

First published 2009 by Routledge
2 Park Square, Milton Park, Abingdon, Oxon, OX14 4RN

Simultaneously published in the USA and Canada
by Routledge
270 Madison Avenue, New York, NY 10016

Routledge is an imprint of the Taylor & Francis Group, an informa business

© 2009 Edited by William Miller and Rita M. Pellen

Typeset in Times by Value Chain, India
Printed and bound in Great Britain by CPI Antony Rowe, Chippenham, Wiltshire.

British Library Cataloguing in Publication Data
A catalogue record for this book is available from the British Library

ISBN10: 0-415-48379-4 (h/b)
ISBN10: 0-415-48381-6 (p/b)
ISBN13: 978-0-415-48379-7 (h/b)
ISBN13: 978-0-415-48381-0 (p/b)

CONTENTS

Introduction:
Living with Google

William Miller

As I write this, I am eagerly awaiting the completion of Siva Vaidhyanathan's book, to be called *The Googlization of Everything: How One Company Is Disrupting Culture, Commerce, and Community–and Why We Should Worry*, the creation of which is being chronicled on his blog, www.googlizationofeverything.com. As discussed in the September 25, 2007 edition of *The Chronicle of Higher Education*, Vaidhyanathan asserts now that Google has "'utterly infiltrated our culture' . . . it's time to start asking questions about Google-as-monolith." He further states that "if Google becomes the dominant way we navigate the Internet . . . then it will have remarkable power to set agendas and alter perceptions. . . . Its biases are built into its algorithms. It knows more about us every day. We know almost nothing about it."

Librarians certainly share these concerns, and many of the authors included in this book are asking questions, though few would want to go back to a pre-Google age. It is fair to say that we in libraries have a love/hate relationship with Google at this point, watching with a mixture of admiration and discomfort as it inexorably displaces our searching tools, and even ourselves to some extent, while on the other hand it makes our lives easier and in any case is an inevitability we need to accept in a creative way and work into our own reconceptualized work, even if we have misgivings about it.

Several Chapters in this book engage in just the sort of questioning that Vaidhyanathan envisions. Charlie Potter very thoughtfully critiques the company and its products in "Standing on the Shoulders of

Libraries: A Holistic and Rhetorical Approach to Teaching Google Scholar." He points out that "Google Scholar succeeds only because libraries have provided access to their resources via the Google Scholar interface," and that libraries "make possible the success of the Google Scholar interface by enabling users to access local collections." Potter advocates that we "look critically and rhetorically at the Google technology itself." He worries that "while librarians claim to stand for access, they are simultaneously allowing an advertising corporation to craftily place itself directly between the library and the patron."

In a similar spirit but in a broader context, Mark Y. Herring cautions us to remember the true value of libraries in his "Fool's Gold: Why the Internet Is No Substitute for a Library." He says "I am certain that I do not want Dante with an ad for Virago, or one for erectile dysfunction." "There may still be time," he says, "to make the Web what it should be, a tool, like many other tools, that can aid and abet our pursuit of turning information into knowledge . . . but the present state of affairs put us exactly light-years from this goal. Are librarians paying any attention to these things? . . . A few more years down this road and the question will no longer matter. We will have, not the future we want, but the future we allowed. We have arrived on the Information Superhighway, all right, but are we rushing all too fast to make libraries, and library services, that highway's first roadkill?"

Two articles take a more positive approach to living with Google. In "Who Holds the Keys to the Web for Libraries?," Emily F. Blankenship acknowledges that "the general public and many librarians now rely upon mega search engines to locate, in a timely manner, the most obscure data." She maintains that "libraries could still play vital roles in these transactions because we can provide access to more scholarly resources, but the mega search engines, in reality, serve as Internet guideposts for most people and our challenge is to bring people back to their library holdings and services." Similarly, in "An Opportunity, Not a Crisis: How Google Is Changing the Individual and the Information Profession," Kay Cahill argues that "much of what is typically seen as negative about Google is, in fact, positive."

Google Scholar and Google Book Search continue to be the focus of most librarians' interest in Google's products, and the lack of information and transparency regarding these products is widespread. Some insight is provided by Barbara Quint in her reprinted piece "Changes at Google Scholar: A Conversation with Anurag Acharya." Quint, an editor at *Searcher* magazine, interviewed the designer of Google Scholar and shares new information such as the fact that Google Scholar "has launched its own digitization project, separate from the high-profile Google Book Search," the fact that it has a new key author feature, and the fact that it is expanding into non-English languages and non-Western content. Quint's article is interesting in light of Philipp Mayr and Anne-Kathrin Walter's earlier findings, in "Studying Journal Coverage in Google Scholar," that there is a paucity of coverage of German literature "as well as weaknesses in the accessibility of Open Access content."

A pair of articles here investigates the practical use of Google Scholar, and librarians' attitudes toward it. In "Attitudes of OhioLINK Librarians Toward Google Scholar™," Joan Giglierano reports the results of a survey of Ohio academic librarians investigating their "attitudes and current practices regarding promotion of Google Scholar." She notes the concerns of some that promoting Scholar will cause users to abandon more traditional library search tools, will lead users to think of librarians as irrelevant, will lead users into a world of "incomplete and redundant content that will water down scholarship," and will, finally, lead users to pay for content that their libraries already provide free of charge. Nevertheless, a minority of Ohio academic institutions are recognizing the tool's value and are linking to it from their Web sites. In "Using Google Scholar at the Reference Desk," Karen Bronshteyn and Kathryn Tvaruzka maintain that Google Scholar has usefulness as a reference tool of last resort, including citation completion, an alternative when catalogs are down, and a helpful resource to encourage interdisciplinary searching.

Google Book Search continues to fascinate librarians. Several pieces here explore this project, in relation to other digitization projects. Jill E. Grogg and Beth Ashmore discuss the relationship between the digitization projects that the Google Book Search partner libraries worked on and how these libraries will use the digital copies of the books scanned by Google. Shawn Martin, in "To Google or Not to Google, That Is the Question: Supplementing Google Book Search to Make It More Useful for Scholarship," discusses the relationship between Google Book Search and Early English Books Online, Evans Early American Imprints, and Eighteenth Century Collections Online Text Creation Partnership, which do a highly specialized full-text-searchable digitization of early English works not amenable to mass digitization because of their gothic or other fonts and other issues surrounding the digitization of nonmodern texts. In "The Million Book Project in Relation to Google" Gloriana St. Clair discusses several digitization projects including The Million Book Project, which is digitizing non-Western materials, UN publications, and other specialized materials not envisioned by Google. In "Using Metadata to

Discover the Buried Treasure in Google Book Search," Millie Jackson explores "the metadata that Google captures as well as comparing it to the MBooks project at The University of Michigan." She discovers that Google facilitates research in many ways, despite its limitations.

Two pieces focusing on little-known Google products round out this collection. In "Google Video–Just Another Video Sharing Site?" Tine Walczyk discusses both Google Video and YouTube, along with other video-sharing resources such as iFilm, AOL, and Broadcaster, as a service to people, and in "Google's Bid to Build Cooperation and Partnerships Through Librarian Central and Google for Educators," Robert J. Lackie points out that Google has made good-faith efforts to create tools to help librarians and educators, which it absolutely had no obligation to do and which we need to become more aware of. The existence of these tools illustrates both Google's constantly expanding restlessness and its sincere desire to reach out, though one could certainly put a sinister spin on these or any other tools which Google has created or will create, and believe that these are merely efforts to co-opt, or "monetize" at some future point.

Love it or hate it, we are learning to live with Google, and we must do so. Perhaps we can also affect Google, if we offer constructive advice, as well as adapting and learning from its more positive aspects. As the cliché goes, librarians like to search, while people like to find, and Google makes it remarkably easy, not always but very often, for us to find things. We are already learning that lesson as we unveil new generations of browsers and online catalogs such as AquaBrowser, Primo, and Endeca. The articles in this collection show that skepticism is healthy and normal, but wholesale rejectionism is counterproductive and unworthy of the best in librarianship. Google is imperfect but it is very helpful. Let us make the most of it, in the spirit of helping our users, which is, after all, what we are about.

Standing on the Shoulders of Libraries: A Holistic and Rhetorical Approach to Teaching Google Scholar

Charlie Potter

The professed goals of the Google Corporation closely resemble those of most public and academic libraries. The stated goal of Google, "to organize the world's information and make it universally accessible and useful," is global in scope and operates on the assumption that, indeed, the world's information is not universally accessible and useful . . . or organized.[1] Of course, no library would claim that it has achieved (or ever could achieve) this lofty goal; one central reason for this is that libraries generally serve local populations (i.e., community members, students, scholars) and/or collect specific materials. In addition to organizing localized collections of information in an attempt to make them accessible and useful, librarians help people find high-quality and apt information depending on their unique search needs, assist information seekers in understanding and using this information, and hope to help people appreciate the value of information seeking with respect to lifelong learning.

Google, in contrast, offers one-stop information shopping and banks on the usability of its interface and ability to generate advertising revenue. Although slight superficial differences exist between the missions of Google and libraries, one still wonders, "Why would a corporation want to step in and do the same thing that a library does, except on a more global scale?" There are several possible answers to this question. First, Google believes (and not altogether unfairly) that it can do a better job of organizing information than librarians can. Second, perhaps, Google also feels that it can enable the creation of information by users across the globe. A third and often unmentioned reason is that Google discovered that it could capitalize on information seekers, especially those who make a career out of research.

Google Scholar, unlike many of Google's more global services, functions in conjunction with another party; in this case, the other party is the academic library (and their local collections). As Google acknowledges, Google Scholar succeeds only because libraries have provided access to their resources via the Google Scholar interface. In addition to the aforementioned goal of organizing the world's information, Google adds the following statement to its Google Scholar help page: "Facilitating library access to scholarly texts brings us one step closer to this goal. We're thankful to the libraries and librarians who make it possible."[2]

Indeed, libraries do make possible the success of the Google Scholar interface by enabling users to access local collections. As Jeffery Pomerantz suggests, "It is possible for libraries to add value to search technologies by providing a layer of service available to those using it."[3] Value, in this case, is evidenced through an endorsement or the employment of a particular search technology; by allowing Google Scholar to link to library resources, libraries have provided the needed "layer of service" that translates into an endorsement of Google.

It is worth noting that Google Scholar has similarly added a layer of service to libraries by allowing people to access materials through a Web-based interface. Google Scholar, at this moment in time, cannot fulfill its stated goal without the help (and financial contribution) of libraries. Thus, although librarians endorse Google and its scholarly search interface, Google claims to make library resources more accessible. Of course, Google also uses the relationship to gain recognition for the Google brand, which in turn creates revenue for the Google Corporation.

For fans of Google, these facts might raise the question, "If Google Scholar gives me what I need, why should I care if they make a little money in the deal, especially since Google Scholar does not yet contain advertisements?" I will examine the implications of this question, highlighting reasons why librarians, especially those involved in bibliographic instruction, need to examine the rhetoric behind Google Scholar and the market forces surrounding it. Using issues of advertising, privacy, and censorship as examples, I will holistically and rhetorically analyze Google Scholar, illustrating that many of the goals and actions of Google are antithetical to those most libraries would support. Further, I will examine the Google Scholar interface and suggest that treating Google technology as a neutral tool is dangerous, as the rhetoric of Google Scholar is shaping a new generation of researchers; in this case, the interface is determining the search. In addition, I will offer possible pedagogical strategies for dealing with Google Scholar in the information literacy curriculum.

LIBRARIES AND GOOGLE SCHOLAR: A MUTUALLY BENEFICIAL RELATIONSHIP?

In many cases, the relationship between libraries and Google Scholar is happily symbiotic. Google Scholar helps the library by lending its popular search technology to the cause of academic research, and libraries allow Google Scholar access to their holdings. The only thing that differs between what one would find in a library database versus what one could find on Google Scholar is, largely, the interface.[4] However, many additional implications emerge from this union. Specifically, as mentioned above, libraries are effectively endorsing the Google Corporation. Of course, corporate endorsements happen frequently in the academic world. As early as the 1960s, critics like Richard Hofstadter began noting the relationship between the university and the corporation. In most cases, this means that a university chooses a Coca-Cola contract over a Pepsi contract or that its sports teams wear Nike rather than Adidas attire. In turn, a university reaps a financial benefit, in addition to other product-related perks.[5]

In the case of libraries and Google Scholar, the corporation provides a service that supplements (or replaces) a service performed previously by the university. Google Scholar does not charge libraries for this service; instead, the library pays in other ways, namely through their agreements with proprietary databases and their purchase of link resolver technology, which I will discuss in a later paragraph. Money does not flow between Google and libraries. Thus, by allowing Google access to their collections, libraries assume the expense of the technology and the scholarly information that make the Google interface successful. In short, the library allows Google to provide access to information for which the library has already paid through a technology that the library provides; in turn, Google also gets an opportunity to advertise for its other sources and a forum through which it can focus solely on interface rather than content.

Of course, we must not forget that Google is, at the end of the day, an advertising corporation–not a public service. This situation is not altogether beneficial for the library when Google, as previously discussed, professes a mission that assumes librarians are not doing an adequate job and need assistance from a corporation. Fears of corporate takeover coupled with fears of being viewed as outdated and obsolete put libraries in a complex ethical and economic quagmire: Do librarians pair with Google and appear to be on the cutting edge of search technology, or do they choose to continue autonomously at the risk of being viewed as an out-of-touch profession of Luddites?

To answer this question, librarians must analyze the value of the Google relationship from the perspective of the user. The best librarians are keenly aware of information equity issues, and a stated goal of the profession is to assuage these concerns. In fact, access and information equity are listed as "core values" of the library profession.[6] As librarians know, one major obstacle to access and equity is the cost of the equipment and interfaces that provide access to that information. Thus, it is a professional ethical imperative that good librarians will offer the *best* information solutions to people, even if those solutions can be obtained without direct use of the proprietary resources of the library. In other words, if Google is seemingly cost-free and provides easy-to-access information (sometimes the same information a person could find in a library, especially in the case of Google Scholar) through an interface users prefer, then librarians must use/teach/recommend Google.

However, good librarians must also ask what factors make something the "best" information source. In addition to the traditional evaluative factors used to determine the quality of an information source, information economics must be considered. Corporations like Google have a significant stake in whether or not resources like Google Scholar will be viewed as viable information resources for academic researchers. When academic libraries add value to Google Scholar by allowing an advertising corporation to dictate the medium through which people find information, they must also ask, to reference Marshall McLuhan, what message is being conveyed through the search medium. For this reason, a holistic rhetorical evaluation–a thorough critique and examination of the linguistic, social, cultural, economic, technological, and political aspects of an entity itself as well as the forces that govern it–can help libraries decide if the values of libraries and their people mesh with the values of the Google corporation.

Samuel Green suggested over 100 years ago that, "A librarian should be as unwilling to allow an inquirer to leave the library with his question unanswered as a shop-keeper is to have a customer go out of his store without making a purchase."[7] Unfortunately, this metaphor is more dangerous than ever; in fact, when one considers Google Scholar, the relationship between "inquirer" and "customer" seems to suggest that the entities are identical or interchangeable rather than metaphorical. An information seeker and a customer looking to make a purchase are not the same; further, a shop-keeper might want to, for personal benefit, sell something to a customer that he/she does not really want or need in order to make a profit. Although Google Scholar is, on the surface, seemingly free to users, it actually resembles the store in the above metaphor, rather than the library. In this case, what appears to be "free" does not always actually promote equity or access. Nor is it truly free.

THE RHETORIC OF GOOGLE SCHOLAR AND THE GOOGLE ENDORSEMENT IMPLICATIONS

The Internet is not neutral or without cost, and neither are the technologies that make it possible. Instead, it is shaped by largely corporate and capitalist forces. As Laura Gurak writes:

> The efficiency of the Internet is great, and the ability to reach out to others and tap into vast sources of information and ideas . . . is profound. Yet more and more of the Internet is being used to make money, gather our personal information, protect corporate intellectual property, and encourage us to shop. . . . How we view the world and how we live in it are being shaped by the features of these new technologies.[8]

Google promotes all of the activities Gurak mentions: making money, gathering information, protecting the corporation over the user, and encouraging consumption through advertising. This is the major way in which the true mission of Google differs from that of most libraries in America.[9] In other words, both entities profess information access and organization as their goals; however, we must ask, "To what end?" For libraries, the answer varies but usually involves fostering an environment where a more intelligent and informed public can grow. Conversely, the answer for Google is making money for itself and its advertisers–seamlessly. We should also not be fooled into thinking that the technology used by Google (or any search technology, really) is a neutral force in the information seeking process. Cynthia Selfe and Gail Hawisher intelligently caution against this type of assumption by pointing out that computers are not simply innocent tools that we use to manipulate or create information; instead, computers and the interfaces they present both shape us and use us to create information.

Data mining, a practice which Google uses to create advertising profiles, is a good example of this phenomenon. A user searches for a product using a particular strategy. He/she finds the product and moves on to another task. All the while, computers and corporations take this data and use them to assemble descriptions of how people search and for what they are searching. Then, a corporation like Google can "combine personal information collected from you with information from other Google services or third parties to provide a better user experience, including customizing content for you."[10] Thus, while a person *thinks* he/she is just doing a basic Google search, he/she is also allowing Google to use information (in conjunction with information from third parties that are likely to also use data mining) from that search to create his/her experience. In other words, an information seeker tells the computer to search for something (i.e., the user is the agent) but the search paradigm has been predetermined. Of course, Google claims to do this for the benefit of information users; however, in reality, the user experience is only important insofar as it supports Google's larger goal: generating money for shareholders.

A conflict of interest exists here, as advertising is a form of persuasion attached solely to selling products and making money; being able to see through this type of persuasion is central to critical literacy and information literacy. I am not the first to argue that Google's true goals actually inhibit the growth of an intelligent and informed public.[11] As John Harms and Douglas Kellner astutely assert:

> [A]dvertising's current role in society is exploitative, wasteful, and manipulative and represents a form of domination that perpetuates capitalist hegemony and that thwarts participatory democracy and the development of individual autonomy.... Advertising undermines the psycho-cultural base for a public sphere and democratic participation in social life. While democracy requires an active, inquiring public citizen/subject, advertising is part of a privatized consumer society which offers commodity spectacles as a substitute for participation in social life. .... Advertising attempts to assure and assuage its audience and to promote the belief that individual commodity solutions are present for all problems.[12]

In other words, advertising, by creating a picture of what people should be by suggesting what they should buy, lulls citizens into passivity. Advertising tells people what to do, rather than encouraging them to think for themselves. Moreover, the capitalist forces that underlie advertising seek to convince people that they are always lacking something and that they need to consume in order to be happy, intelligent, and/or acceptable. Advertising assumes that the way to act is to consume rather than to, say, protest or learn. By attaching advertising and persuasion (very libidinal persuasion, in most cases) to information seeking, Google emphasizes that participation is most important when it involves spending money.

As previously mentioned, Google Scholar does not currently include advertisements in its list of results. However, Google has not eliminated the possibility of ads on Google Scholar pages. In a 2005 article, a Google Scholar engineer was asked about the possibility of advertising on Google Scholar. His response was non-committal: "It's possible down the line."[13] This is to be expected; libraries are not paying for the use of this service, and, for reasons previously discussed, the library profession would be naïve to think that Google is offering this service without the possibility of making some money.

Regardless of absence of product advertising on the pages of Google Scholar at the time of the publication of this chapter, the most obvious advertisement lies within Google Scholar itself: each page is marked with a giant Google logo–the most obvious endorsement that libraries give the Google Corporation. This is what makes the Google Scholar interface attractive; it is branded with a familiar name that users already know and trust. Conversely, when a user searches a library website or proprietary database, he/she might be encountering a new brand. This argument relates to the success of federated searching more generally. People prefer to use as few interfaces as possible. Some information professionals suggest that libraries should not even possess websites; rather, they should work as diligently as possible to integrate seamlessly with other services, namely Google Scholar. Lorcan Dempsey, for example, argues for this type of integration, specifically because services like Google Scholar reach "learners where they choose to look for information."[14] This way, learners will eventually find themselves searching through library content, even if they did not initially start at the website of the library. However, when we are "meeting" learners in a space not controlled by the library, we are condoning and promoting the use of that space, however indirectly. Google Scholar is indeed advertising for its more general search services, which, of course, advertise to generate revenue. In this way, Google Scholar is currently a piece of a much larger revenue pie, and intelligent users cannot ignore what the larger Google Corporation does (or why they do it), especially when the Google Scholar service all the while understates the involvement of libraries and other proprietary databases.[15]

Thus, Google is funded by advertisements, and these same advertisements inadvertently make Google Scholar possible. Further, the cost of a service like Google Scholar is hidden because of the absence of ads paired with the fact that Google is an advertising corporation. As Stephen Best and Douglas Kellner suggest, "Consumers pay for the spectacles of entertainment, subsidized by advertising, in the form of higher costs for products. Moreover, the entertainment and information offered is a function of what the culture industries think will sell and that on the whole advances its own interests, producing more desires for its goods and way of life."[16] In this case, the interests of the culture industry are likely counter to the larger purpose of the library.

While I cannot argue that *any* information or institution is truly neutral–everything is indeed rhetorical on some level–or free from bias or persuasion, I believe that certain transgressions of neutrality should not be overlooked. For example, Google was recently publicly criticized for its response to Michael Moore's documentary on the wrongdoings of the pharmaceutical industry, *Sicko*. On the Google Health Advertising blog,[17] blogger Lauren Turner authored an entry entitled, "Does negative press make you Sicko?"[18] In the post, Turner acknowledges that the film is "generating significant buzz and is sure to spur a lively conversation about health coverage, care, and quality in America. While legislators, litigators, and patient groups are growing excited, others among us are growing nervous."

It's easy to read between the lines here: the people who are growing nervous are the pharmaceutical, health care, and advertising companies. Why? They have been criticized and stand to lose money. Whether one believes the highly rhetorical strategies of *Sicko* (which is also a money-generating product), he/she must also be aware that Google is prepared to defend the pharmaceutical industry with–what else?–advertisements. Turner continues,

> We can place text ads, video ads, and rich media ads in paid search results or in relevant websites within our ever-expanding content network. Whatever the problem, Google can act as a platform for educating the public and promoting your message. We help you connect your company's assets while helping users find the information they seek.

Thus, Google is trying to, as Turner notes, "solve the problems" of Big Pharma using ads. Users should note that this is not a public service campaign. Instead, it is one corporation looking to protect another. Essentially, Google has said to pharmaceutical and health care corporations, "Tell us what you want us to say about your corporation, and we will say it, if you pay us enough." This blog illustrates no concern for honesty or the integrity of information.

This health information-related incident highlights several problems with Google Scholar and the larger Google enterprise. Health information is an example commonly used by librarians and other information literacy educators to illustrate the dangers of the Internet. For example, the website of the National Network of Libraries of Medicine explicitly states, "Be aware that websites which advertise products should be read with great care."[19] The National Institutes of Health provides similar guidelines.[20]

In this instance, a dichotomy exists between the information one finds on Google versus Google Scholar. One is profit-driven and contains advertisements, and the other is seemingly benign. Some Internet users are savvy enough to know that they should not trust *just any* website for their health information, and academic librarians attempt to teach users how to evaluate websites for their credibility when it comes to matters of health; however, these users have access to reliable proprietary health information through their academic library. In this situation, the inference made by Google is that one source of information is reputable; the other source contains information with varying levels of dependability. Thus, the information in Google Scholar is good, and the information found through the original Google interface may be bad (or, at least, librarians would caution users against it due to its advertisements which are often biased toward pharmaceutical and health care companies).

It is important to ask whether, as information practitioners, we can in good conscience refer users to a tool that is owned and operated with the revenue that is potentially generated by these kinds of profit-driven advertisements that are, in some cases, only loosely based on truth. We must also question whether it is acceptable for a search interface to include advertisements but not acceptable for a website to do so. When we suggest Google without pointing out to users that it is indeed a website that advertises products, are we not ignoring our own advice regarding information literacy? And what if we cannot suggest Google Scholar because our university is not affiliated or a user is not affiliated with a university? Further, is it ethical for Google to provide two products: one with "unsafe" information and advertisements, and one with scholarly information and no advertisements?[21]

We must give equal consideration to the privacy practices of the Google Corporation. Intellectual freedom and privacy are hallmarks of the library profession. Librarians have been some of the only professionals to, as an organization, oppose the privacy-violating aspects of the U.S. PATRIOT Act and are generally in support of legislation that promotes the rights of individuals to read about and search for information on virtually every topic. Despite this commitment to privacy, the interaction that occurs between librarian and patron has been thought to sometimes inhibit possible search questions over controversial topics, whereas the impersonal Internet provides anonymity and the freedom to search for any topic, however lewd, dangerous, or personal. Of course, whether people know it or not, this is simply untrue. While the embarrassment of asking certain questions might inhibit users, one can easily argue that what they don't know *is hurting them.*

Google has been criticized repeatedly concerning its policy of retaining search records indefinitely.[22] Curious about communism? Google knows. Have a debilitating and personal disease? Google knows. Of course, institutions like Google could use this information to, say, catch child predators or terrorists. However, this type of surveillance is frightening, especially because most people are so unaware of the digital trail that follows every search. The people who are aware can be scared into ignorance, choosing not to research certain subjects because of their social or political import. Although it is worth noting that many of the major proprietary databases do not publicly disclose their practices for retaining search records,[23] one cannot ignore these privacy issues while using Google Scholar, especially considering Google's status as a major advertising corporation.

Google recently acquired the Double Click corporation in a deal that is currently under investigation for anti-trust violations by the Federal Trade Commission. Using cookies, Double Click helps Google track not only the ads you view but also the websites you visit.[24] As noted in *The New York Times*, the argument against Google is, essentially, that the acquisition of Double Click will "give one company access to more information about the Internet activities of consumers than any other company in the world."[25] Even if Google Scholar is Google's innocent ad-free side project, should we not be concerned about supporting a corporation whose goal is to acquire information about its users in order to advertise to them? It is worth noting that Google Scholar has the same privacy policy as Google. There is no guarantee that cookies will not be placed on your computer; even if you are not looking at advertisements directly, information about you might be gathered for advertising purposes. Further, if we are concerned about intellectual freedom, should we also not be concerned about supporting corporations with anti-trust issues?

A third conflict of interest between libraries and Google involves the censoring of search results through the Google Chinese interface. When Google discovered that, mysteriously, Google was not working properly in China, the corporation agreed to create a separate Google service for the country that removed "certain sensitive information from [the] search results."[26] In this case, sensitive information means information that Chinese officials find inappropriate, dangerous, or unpalatable. Andrew McLaughlin, senior policy counsel for the Google Corporation, stated, "Filtering our search results clearly compromises our mission. Failing to offer Google search at all to a fifth of the world's population, however, does so far more severely."[27] A rhetorical look at this statement reveals several things. First, Google thinks its product to be more important than the principles of intellectual freedom and access, two of its professed goals. Google claims to want to make the world's information accessible but then agrees to censor it in favor of market opportunities. China is easily the world's fastest growing economy, and Google felt that capitalizing on this factor was more important that holding to its professed mission. Interestingly, McLaughlin then states:

We aren't happy about what we had to do this week, and we hope that over time everyone in the world will come to enjoy full access to information. But how is that full access most likely to be achieved? We are convinced that the Internet, and its continued development through the efforts of companies like Google, will effectively contribute to openness and prosperity in the world.

Google is thus implying that it *had to* do this; its product is so valuable, how could it let one-fifth of the world's population do without? Further, Google believes that, indeed, it will be Google and its technology that bring "openness and prosperity to the world"–even if in doing so it supports censorship. If Google had not agreed to create a Google site for China, then it would have been complicit in a far worse kind of censorship–a market censorship that kept the Chinese from the products they want (or need, according to Google). Thus, it is okay to censor ideas but not okay to censor the market.

One of the great flaws in Google's reasoning is the idea that technology, specifically digital technology, is the centerpiece around which all knowledge and "progress" revolve. This philosophy is known as technological determinism and privileges technology as the most important factor in progress. As Frank Webster notes, this is viewed by many scholars as a dangerous strategy because "it relegates into an entirely separate division social, economic, and political dimensions of technological innovation. These follow from, and are subordinate to, the premier league of technology which appears to be self-perpetuating, though it leaves its impress on all aspects of society."[28] One can easily see how this devolves into a chicken-egg issue: Which came first–did society/economy/politics/etc., determine technology, or did technology come first? Of course, this complicates the argument that the introduction of new search technologies into China will inevitably improve freedom of information. Further, the stance taken by Google on this issue closely resembles an argument for exporting democracy. In other words, Google argues that China does not know what is best for China–an American corporation does. Essentially, Google suggests that a capitalist American search engine has the power to bring democracy to China; if the Chinese can shop (because, at this point, they cannot use Google to think critically or find critical information) and find out about products through Google, then they will become better capitalists and better citizens. If librarians are going to endorse Google in any way, but specifically through a contractual relationship with Google Scholar, they must recognize and contemplate the ways that these issues undermine the very bedrock of the library profession.

We must also look critically and rhetorically at the Google technology itself. As suggested previously, librarians add value to Google when they teach students how to use Google Scholar. Of course, the information presented in the databases has value in and of itself; however, it is, generally, the academic library that facilitates access to this information through link resolver technology (It is worth noting that this is costly technology that libraries carry the burden of purchasing. Google does not share the cost of these types of technologies with libraries.). The citations seen by on-campus users are considerably different from those seen by users affiliated with a campus, as on-campus users see a direct link to their institution's library in a result that is locally held. Users not located on a campus but who are affiliated with a campus can activate the links provided by their library through the Google interface. After doing this, users will be able to access the available articles through the remote access authentication provided by their institution. However, if users are unaware of this technology or unaffiliated with a university, they are led to believe that they must purchase the article in order to obtain it. In reality, most of these items could be obtained by going to the local academic or public library and viewing the items on on-campus computers. In addition, the articles that cannot be obtained by a library can usually be found using interlibrary loan, a service free to those affiliated with most universities or public libraries. However, users who are presented with the option of paying for an article would generally make the choice to do so based on one of two factors: either the individual desires to pay for the convenience of not having to go to the library (or activate the library links through Google Scholar) or he/she is unaware of the services/information offered by the library. While the latter is arguably the responsibility of libraries themselves, the former factor is quite problematic when one considers that a user could sometimes be paying $50 or more for an article from the British Library or a publisher.

This begs the question: Who is responsible for making sure that information seekers do not purchase information that is already available to them? Libraries are built upon the premise of providing information equally to all users.[29] In other words, if a person needs access to an expensive article, he/she can visit an academic or public library and pick up what he/she needs without paying for the item specifically in most cases. Conversely, Google is a for-profit corporation that serves to make money off of its services. Although Google claims not to take a cut of the money spent by users who choose to purchase articles through Google Scholar, Google uses its search technology to capitalize on services for which libraries are already paying. If users are familiar with

the concept that information on the Internet is not free (the music industry and downloading are an example), they are likely to pay for individual articles, *if they can afford it*. Moreover, one could easily argue that
anyone who purchases an article through the Google Scholar interface
is indeed paying twice: once through Google, and once through either
taxes or tuition.[30] In this way, Google Scholar reinforces class divisions
that libraries seek to dissolve. The very notion that Google Scholar and
Google offer services that differ based on their intellectual weight is indeed classist. At this time, Google Scholar is not pairing with public libraries to provide access to their more scholarly resources. Thus, if
people are affiliated with a university, they can access the "good" and
reputable information through Google Scholar. If they are not, they can
read some advertisements while sifting through websites that may or not
be relevant or reliable.

The model of television programming provides an interesting point
of comparison here. In a discussion of the work of Herbert Schiller,
Webster discusses the impacts of information stratification on the types
of information provided by television corporations:

> [M]ass sales are essential since each household is, in relative terms,
> a poor source of revenue for the information industry. Given this,
> those addressing the domestic realm must aim to supply a mass
> market, since it is only when individual homes are aggregated as
> the "general public" that they have any real market attraction. Once
> they are aggregated, however, the "general public" must be offered
> information products which are undifferentiated–hence the famil-
> iar television monitor and the plethora of game and chat shows,
> soaps, movies, and sport. Further, the "general public" has proven
> itself reluctant to pay anything direct for television program-
> ming–that has been subsidized by the advertiser and/or sponsor.[31]

Of course, some aspects of this comparison do not fit. For example, it is
unlikely that the existence of Google Scholar is going to "dumb down"
research (It might, however, make possible the distribution of less reputable research, unfinished manuscripts, etc. Scholars like Jonathan
Rochkind have explored this concept.[32]). However, the mass distribution
of scholarly research is, according to a capitalist model, essential because
individual researchers, like individual television-watching households,
are worthless when it comes to information industry revenue. This is because, simply put, no matter how many individual articles researchers
might purchase, their contributions will never provide as much money as

advertising revenue. This creates a need for information stratification. Further, individual researchers must be homogenized in order to create a market niche that can be adequately addressed in the marketplace. Thus, researchers are being "aggregated" as the "general researching public" so that they become a greater market attraction.

This idea is supported by the fact that conducting an Advanced Search of Google Scholar still yields quite broad results. Péter Jacsó has highlighted this fact in a comprehensive review of Google Scholar, stating that, "Its search engine often returns inflated and strange hit numbers and citedness scores; does not offer elementary search options for scholarly research; and presents the search results in a discombobulating format, such as mistaking citing journal for cited journal, citing year for cited year and chapter titles for author names."[33] These observations illustrate the fact that Google Scholar is indeed a site that tries to accommodate all researchers using the same search interface and the same types of results. In fact, the site does not offer the most basic of scholarly search options, the option to limit to peer-reviewed items. The Advanced Search function, for example, allows users to limit their searches by the following broad subject areas:

- Biology, Life Sciences, and Environmental Science
- Business, Administration, Finance, and Economics
- Chemistry and Materials Science
- Engineering, Computer Science, and Mathematics
- Medicine, Pharmacology, and Veterinary Science
- Physics, Astronomy, and Planetary Science
- Social Sciences, Arts, and Humanities

These subject areas are comparable to the areas represented in a large, general database likely to be found in an academic library (e.g., Academic Index, Academic Search Premier). Conversely, a search of a specific library database—say, Philosopher's Index—will produce comparatively narrow results with even a basic search. As Rochkind notes, one cannot be sure of the lack of exhaustivity in Google Scholar.[34] In other words, a researcher cannot know, as he/she does when searching a library database, what is or is not included in a list of Google Scholar results. Nor does a librarian know. The Google results are, in many ways, "undifferentiated," at least in the eyes of the amateur information searcher. Like television viewers, the "general researching public" does not prefer to pay by article (although Google Scholar may trick it into doing so, as previously suggested) but will not even wince at the idea of paying through advertising. The message Google Scholar sends is that "undifferentiated" research meets the needs of the "general researching public." Thus, Google determines what researchers need and applies this determination to *all* researchers, no matter the discipline.

The homogenization of researchers raises additional concerns related to our conceptions of the definition of a researcher. Interestingly, Google claims that "Google Scholar aims to sort articles the way researchers do, weighing the full text of each article, the author, the publication in which the article appears, and how often the piece has been cited in other scholarly literature." Although this statement suggests that Google attempts to understand and accommodate the "average" Google Scholar user, it makes totalizing assumptions about how people look for information. Any librarian knows that the search process can vary widely from user to user and discipline to discipline. Although Google Scholar might think that it has developed a more "organic" brand of searching, a closer look reveals that, as Cynthia Selfe and Richard Selfe, Jr., have argued, assumptions like the ones made by Google Scholar pose significant theoretical problems with respect to the purpose of their interface.[35] Primarily, Google Scholar, aside from its single search box screen, offers one advanced search interface, as illustrated above. Conversely, most proprietary databases purchased through the library provide a complex hyperlinked thesaurus that can be used for subject searching, among other searching options. Further, these databases often allow users the option of browsing through journal issues. In other words, while one cannot claim that these databases can accommodate *every* user, at least these databases acknowledge that there is not a "typical" kind of researcher and accordingly attempt to provide results in varying formats. Moreover, the indexing of a library database is transparent, and the indexing of Google Scholar is opaque at best.

Here, it becomes obvious that Google is, indeed, creating a new and hazardous kind of searching–what has been called "good enough" searching by many librarians.[36] Of course, when it comes to scholarly researchers, the idea of "good enough" searching becomes much more serious. Authors like Selfe and Selfe have argued that this kind of homogenization of users can, at times, exhibit a disconcerting bias toward one "correct" kind of searching that is both isolating and totalizing.[37] Thus, by trying to closely mimic what they believe to be the typical strategies of the "researcher," Google Scholar undermines the concept that searchers are *different*; further, by forcing a homogenous search paradigm onto the researching public, Google Scholar forces researchers into its totalizing mold and encourages them not to seek alternative ways of searching, thereby promoting a philosophy of "our search is good enough–after all, it's modeled on what *researchers* naturally do!"

USING GOOGLE SCHOLAR IN THE CLASSROOM

As Richard Wiggins suggests, libraries must create better search technologies in order to compete with Google Scholar and rid themselves of its more problematic aspects. He notes:

> We must distinguish between the thousands of information professionals–mostly librarians–who did important specialized searches in 1980, versus the millions of people who search Google and other popular search engines in 2006. We can try to persuade the bridge designers, the vaccine makers, and the malaria specialists to go back to relying on their librarian intermediaries. Or the information industry can figure out how to make the good stuff as available and as relevant as a Google search.[38]

This observation astutely points to the fact that libraries must, in the face of Google and other technological changes, fight to stay relevant and useful if they wish to be the medium by which searchers find information. Of course, this is an age-old issue for libraries. Technologies like television and radio also threatened to make the library extinct. Thus, there must be something else at stake here than simple relevance. The library can try to find, as Wiggins suggests, other resources in the "information industry" that do what Google does, presumably sans the advertisements and other conflicts of interest. However, libraries *must* accept the challenge of educating users to think rhetorically about the technologies they use, however seemingly harmless those technologies may be. Although I (as a librarian) have a stake in seeing that libraries continue in one form or another, I would argue that it is less important for libraries to win back their "defectors" than it is for us to educate, through information literacy instruction and other course-integrated initiatives, users to be "technology *critics* as well as technology users."[39]

Here, the distinction between critique and evaluation is essential. A great difference exists between simply evaluating a website based on its domain name and critiquing an interface for its assumptions about research. Further, "[a]n overly optimistic vision of technology is not only reductive, and, thus, inaccurate, it is also dangerous in that it renders less visible the negative contributions of technology that may work potently and effectively against critically reflective habits."[40] In other

words, we cannot simply evaluate the content of websites–we must critique the technology that takes us to those sites. Inherent in this technology are assumptions about what information is good or bad, useful or
useless, and, in the case of Google, profitable or not profitable. In case
of Google Scholar, as previously noted, these assumptions even extend into the realm of who a "researcher" is and what he/she does when
searching. Thus, we must teach students not only to evaluate websites but
also to critique the technologies that enable their information seeking.
Without this vital step, information literacy instruction can be rendered
moot, as it fails to acknowledge that technology itself is *not neutral*.

But how do we actively teach students to criticize tools like Google
Scholar? How can librarians successfully navigate the more problematic issues of these types of search technologies while still "meeting
students where they are" as many information professionals have suggested we should do?[41] After all, most librarians use Google, and many
librarians even use Google Scholar in order to complete reference tasks.
For the reasons mentioned in the previous sections of this chapter,
teaching a tool like Google Scholar that one does not understand or does
not feel to be "information neutral" can be unnerving. The answer, as
I suggested above, lies in helping students understand that one can be
both a user *and* a critic of technology.

Stuart Selber, a scholar of Composition and Rhetoric, provides helpful pedagogical suggestions for teaching technological and rhetorical
critique in the information literacy classroom.[42] Selber recommends asking students to conduct a rhetorical analysis on advanced search engines
and specifying that students should attempt to identify the different types
of discourses that are present. He suggests that an understanding of the
various discourses used in an advanced search engine can help students
understand that they need to master several academic discourses in order
to be savvy searchers.

Building on Selber's ideas, I suggest that students, in addition to thinking about the discourse needed to use a search engine, should spend time
thinking about the rhetorical construction of the search engine itself.
Such an information literacy session might look like this: In groups, students can choose an advanced search engine to analyze and critique.
Groups will help facilitate student discussion and will allow students
with varying expertise to share across varying backgrounds and subject
positions. Students should ask, "What knowledge do I need to have in
order to use this database?" (e.g., a defined subject, the location of the
search engine). Students could then ask what types of tasks one needs to
master before being able to search the database (e.g., how to read, how

to use a mouse). Once inside a list of results, students can conduct a similar kind of analysis.

Then, students can be asked to dig deeper and ask what types of forces determine whether or not they possessed the knowledge or skills to use the database (e.g., education, age, family history, experience with computers). In addition, students should pay close attention to the language used on the page (e.g., does the box say "Search" or "Go"?). Also, students should consider the design of the page (e.g., how many search boxes?). Students should be encouraged to think through *all* of the knowledge, skills, and language they need, including even the most basic of ideas or tasks. Then, students can critique the search engine based on what was assumed and what might not have been considered. For example, if a search engine (like Google Scholar), has only one search box, what does that imply about the targeted user? Also, who runs the site? In turn, who runs the company which runs the site? Is it a for-profit corporation? Does that corporation have other corporate ties? Students then can develop a short report based on their findings. Instructors can also ask students if their opinion of the resource changed. What would make them stop using the resource?

This assignment could be done in conjunction with any number of classes, from introductory to more advanced courses. It could also be conducted by a professor or teacher at the suggestion and advisement of a librarian. Such an assignment encourages students to think about the ways that resources like Google Scholar are not neutral; instead, they can often portray very strong biases and even sometimes contradict certain tenets of democracy and intellectual freedom.

Of course, we must extend our critique beyond Google Scholar and also carefully examine the ways that the proprietary resources of the library (along with librarians themselves) carry implicit and explicit biases about the value of search technologies and the information to which they lead us. However, in the library instruction classroom, critiques of products like Google Scholar are especially important because, although endorsed by libraries, these products are not affiliated with libraries, librarians, or the overarching goals of the profession. My goal is not to create an opposition between "library resources" and "other resources"; however, librarians seek to follow the information literacy standards set forth by the ACRL, while corporations like Google are, at the end of the day, following the bottom line. If information is stuff out of which knowledge is constructed, the library profession cannot ignore the ways in which Google Scholar can shape that information, even in the most seemingly innocuous and unobtrusive ways. Thus, critique of all types of information technologies is essential to creating information-literate and critically literate citizens.

WHO MADE WHOM?

One of the questions Google Scholar presents on its Google help page reads: "Why are you asking us to 'Stand on the shoulders of giants'? Are you really giants?"[43] This slogan, "Stand on the Shoulders of Giants," is an attempt by Google Scholar to recognize that researchers, through the process of reading and using information to engage in age-old debates and to create new arguments, depend upon generations of scholars before them. The response Google posts on this page explains: "Not even close. That phrase is our acknowledgement that much of scholarly research involves building on what others have already discovered. It's taken from Sir Isaac Newton's famous quote, 'If I have seen further, it is by standing on the shoulders of giants.'" The irony of this question is thick. Google has made a conscious choice to include this question in its FAQ, and its answer obliviously omits any reference to the fact that Google Scholar is actually standing on the shoulders of the thousands of libraries that have come before it–libraries that rarely made a profit. Indeed, Google Scholar is not just standing there. It is, for better or worse, actively chipping away at what research once was by making the corporation the gatekeeper to information.

Libraries effectively embody the image of Atlas, the weight of the world on their shoulders. Critique does not always suggest resistance to change, and librarians should acknowledge that Google Scholar is indeed adding more than a "layer of service" to the library; instead, by allowing Google Scholar to stand on our shoulders, we are welcoming the further commodification of information. While librarians claim to stand for access, they are simultaneously allowing an advertising corporation to craftily place itself directly between the library and the user. Recognizing and understanding the additional byproducts and implications of this relationship are central to true information literacy. We cannot, unless we find ways to holistically and rhetorically criticize Google Scholar and the corporate interests it represents, expect that we will not cave under its weight.

NOTES

1. Google Scholar, "Support for Libraries," Google Scholar, <http://scholar. google.com/intl/en/scholar/libraries.html>.

2. Ibid.

3. Jeffery Pomerantz, "Google Scholar and 100 Percent Availability of Information," *Information Technology and Libraries* 25 (2006): 53-54.

4. The results available through Google Scholar may be more or less plentiful, depending on whether a patron has remote access through a local library and how extensively a library's collection is accessible through Google Scholar. Every library is an organic collection, and this is reflected in Google Scholar access. Also, certain open source materials appear on Google Scholar; however, this article will focus solely on the library-based resources.

5. For more information about corporate contracts in universities, see: Eyal Press and Jennifer Washburn, "The Kept University," *Atlantic Monthly* 285, no. 3 (March 2000): 39-54.

6. American Library Association, "Core Values of Librarianship," American Library Association, <http://www.ala.org/ala/oif/statementspols/corevaluesstatement/ covalues.htm#access>.

7. Samuel S. Green, "Personal Relations between Librarians and Readers," *American Library Journal* I, nos. 2-3 (1876): 79.

8. Laura Gurak, *Cyberliteracy: Navigating the Internet with Awareness* (New Haven: Yale, 2001), 10.

9. The author acknowledges that libraries are also not neutral spaces; in fact, he thinks an examination of this fact is very important. While libraries certainly do perpetuate certain values, they are different from Google Scholar in two major ways. First, libraries are not attempting to corner every aspect of the information market, as he will discuss later in the essay. Second, they do not generate income from advertising.

10. For more information, visit: <http://www.google.com/privacypolicy.html# information>.

11. For information about the ways advertising harms society, see: Guy Debord, *Society of the Spectacle* (New York: Zone Books, 1967); Herbert Schiller, *Mass Communications and American Empire* (New York: Westview, 1992); Douglas Kellner and Stephen Best, "Debord and the Postmodern Turn: New Stages of the Spectacle," *Substance* 90, (1999): 129-156.

12. John Harms and Douglas Kellner, "Toward a Critical Theory of Advertising," *Illuminations,* <http://www.uta.edu/huma/illuminations/kell6.htm>.

13. Anurag Acharya quoted in "Google Scholar Links with Libs.," *Library Journal* 130, no. 7 (April 15, 2005): 18.

14. Joan K. Lippincott, "Where Learners Go," *Library Journal* 130, no. 16 (October 1, 2005): 37.

15. It is worth reemphasizing here that no proprietary information resources are neutral. In fact, one could argue that an EBSCOhost icon advertises for other EBSCO services. However, Google is trying to become the main resource for all of the world's information access. In addition to Google Docs, Google Reader, Google Earth, and Google Maps (and this is not a complete list), Google has also acquired YouTube. If librarians were once the centralized gatekeepers of information, then it seems that Google is striving to be the new gatekeeper.

16. Douglas Kellner and Stephen Best, "Debord and the Postmodern Turn: New Stages of the Spectacle," *Substance* 90 (1999): 129-156.

17. In order to keep in contact with its advertisers, Google representatives maintain corporate blogs that serve to inform advertisers about Google news and advertising opportunities or strategies.

18. Lauren Turner, "Does Negative Press Make You Sicko?" Google Health Advertising Blog, http://google-health-ads.blogspot.com/2007/06/does-negative-press- make-you-sicko.html.

19. National Network of Libraries of Medicine, "Health Information on the Web," National Network of Libraries of Medicine, <http://nnlm.gov/hip/#A2>.

20. U.S. National Library of Medicine and the National Institutes of Health, "MedlinePlus Guide to Healthy Web Surfing," MedlinePlus, <http://www.nlm.nih.gov/medlineplus/healthywebsurfing.html>.

21. This predicament has serious class implications, addressed in a later paragraph.

22. For more information on Google's privacy policy, visit: <http://www.google.com/privacypolicy.html#information>. Additionally, Google recently changed the length of time it keeps information attached to search data. Under the new policy, data will become anonymous (identifiers will be removed) more quickly. For more information, visit: <http://googleblog.blogspot.com/2007/06/how-long-should-google-remember.html>.

23. The major difference, however, between privacy concerns related to proprietary databases versus those associated with Google is that Google uses the results to generate revenue through advertising while proprietary databases presumably only use them to change or improve service. For information about the privacy practices of EBSCO, visit <http://web.ebscohost.com/ehost/external?vid=2&hid=2&sid=49cc8ff5-04cf-464a-b5e0-1574d1a5bb32%40SRCSM1>. For similar information about Thomson Gale, visit <http://www.gale.com/epcopyright/index.htm#privacy>.

24. To read more about Double Click's controversial privacy practices, visit <http://www.doubleclick.com/us/about_doubleclick/privacy/>.

25. See Steve Lohr, "Google Deal Said to Bring U. S. Scrutiny," *The New York Times* (May 29, 2007). It should be noted that some of the major proponents of the FTC investigation were Microsoft and AT&T, competitors of Google.

26. Google, "Google in China," Official Google Blog, <http://googleblog.blogspot.com/2006/01/google-in-china.html>.

27. Ibid.

28. Frank Webster, *Theories of the Information Society* (London: Routledge, 2002), 11.

29. Most libraries operate on models of solidarity and sustainability, but users do usually pay for libraries in one way or another. However, the costs associated with paying for access to a library are generally considerably less over time than paying article-by-article through an interface like Google's.

30. Perhaps, users searching through Google have paid a third and fourth time: with the money they are convinced by advertising to spend and with the privacy they surrender when using Google.

31. Webster, 147.

32. Jonathan Rochkind, "(Meta)search Like Google," *Library Journal* 132, no. 3 (February 15, 2007): 28-30.

33. Péter Jacsó, Google Scholar (Redux), "Peter's Digital Reference Shelf," June, 2005.

34. Rochkind, 29.

35. Cynthia Selfe and Richard Selfe, Jr., "The Politics of the Interface: Power and Its Exercise in Electronic Contact Zones," *College Composition and Communication* 45, no. 4 (Dec., 1994), 480-504.

36. For an analysis of this issue, see: Brian Kenney, "Googlizers vs. Resistors," *Library Journal* 129, no. 20 (December 2004), 44-46.

37. Selfe and Selfe.

38. Richard Wiggins, "Latent Value and Perceived Value: Another Expert Opinion," *Searcher* 14, no. 4 (April 2006): 19.

39. Selfe and Selfe, 484.

40. Selfe and Selfe, 482

41. For more information on this concept, see: Anne Lipow, "Serving the Remote User. Reference Service in the Digital Environment," (paper presented at the Ninth Australasian Information Online and On Disc Conference and Exhibition, Sydney, Australia, Jan. 19-21, 1999) <www.csu.edu.au/special/online99/proceedings 99/ 200.htm>.

42. Stuart Selber, *Multiliteracies for a Digital Age* (Carbondale: Southern Illinois, 2004), 58-59.

43. Google Scholar, "Google Scholar Help," Google Scholar, <http://scholar.google.com/intl/en/scholar/help.html>.

REFERENCES

American Library Association. "Core Values of Librarianship." American Library Association. <http://www.ala.org/ala/oif/statementspols/corevaluesstatement/corevalu es.htm#access> (accessed July 31, 2007).

Debord, Guy. *Society of the Spectacle.* New York: Zone Books, 1967.

"Google Scholar Links with Libs." *Library Journal* 130 no. 7 (April 15, 2005): 16-18.

Google Scholar. "Support for Libraries." Google Scholar. <http://scholar.google.com/intl/en/scholar/libraries.html> (accessed July 31, 2007).

Gurak, Laura. *Cyberliteracy: Navigating the Internet with Awareness.* New Haven: Yale, 2001.

Green, Samuel S. "Personal Relations between Librarians and Readers." *American Library Journal I* nos. 2-3 (1876): 74-81.

Harms, John and Douglas Kellner. "Toward a Critical Theory of Advertising." Illuminations. <http://www.uta.edu/huma/illuminations/kell6.htm> (accessed July 31, 2007).

Jacsó, Péter. "Google Scholar (Redux)." *Peter's Digital Reference Shelf* (June, 2005). <http://www.gale.com/servlet/HTMLFileServlet?imprint=9999&region=7&fileName=/reference/archive/200506/google.html> (accessed July 31, 2007).

Kellner, Douglas and Stephen Best. "Debord and the Postmodern Turn: New Stages of the Spectacle." *Substance* 90 (1999): 129-156.

Kenney, Brian. "Googlizers vs. Resistors." *Library Journal* 129, no. 20 (December 2004): 44-46.

Lipow, Anne G. "Serving the Remote User. Reference Service in the Digital Environment," Paper presented at the Ninth Australasian Information Online and On Disc

Conference and Exhibition, Sydney, Australia, Jan. 19-21, 1999. <www.csu.edu. au/special/online99/proceedings99/200.htm> (accessed July 31, 2007).

Lippincott, Joan K. "Where Learners Go." *Library Journal* 130, no. 16 (October 1 2005): 35-37.

McLuhan, Marshall. *The Medium is the Massage: An Inventory of Effects.* New York: Random House, 1967.

National Network of Libraries of Medicine. "Health Information on the Web." National Network of Libraries of Medicine. <http://nnlm.gov/hip/#A2> (accessed July 31, 2007).

Pomerantz, Jeffery. "Google Scholar and 100 Percent Availability of Information." *Information Technology and Libraries* 25 (2006): 52-56.

Press, Eyal and Jennifer Washburn. "The Kept University." *Atlantic Monthly* 285, no. 3 (March 2000): 39-54.

Rochkind, Jonathan. "(Meta)search Like Google." *Library Journal* 132, no. 3 (February 15, 2007): 28-30.

Schiller, Herbert. *Mass Communications and American Empire.* New York: Westview, 1992.

Selber, Stuart. *Multiliteracies for a Digital Age.* Carbondale: Southern Illinois, 2004.

Selfe, Cynthia L. and Richard J. Selfe, Jr. "The Politics of the Interface: Power and Its Exercise in Electronic Contact Zones." *College Composition and Communication* 45, no. 4. (Dec., 1994): 480-504.

Selfe, Cynthia and Gail Hawisher. "The Rhetoric of Technology and the Electronic Writing Class." *College Composition and Communication* 42, no. 1 (1991): 55-65.

Turner, Lauren. "Does Negative Press Make You Sicko?" Google Health Advertising Blog. <http://google-health-ads.blogspot.com/2007/06/does-negative-press-make-you-sicko.html> (accessed July 24, 2007).

U.S. National Library of Medicine and the National Institutes of Health, "MedlinePlus Guide to Healthy Web Surfing," MedlinePlus, <http://www.nlm.nih.gov/medline plus/healthywebsurfing.html> (accessed July 31, 2007).

Webster, Frank. *Theories of the Information Society.* (London: Routledge, 2002).

Wiggins, Richard. "Latent Value and Perceived Value: Another Expert Opinion." *Searcher* 14.4 (April 2006): 19.

Fool's Gold:
Why the Internet
Is No Substitute for a Library

Mark Y. Herring

Naysayers are a peculiar fish, always trying to swim upstream, go against current trends. Look at salmon, for instance. Upstream for all their lives and then what: shotten herring as it were. Surely those who presume to swim upstream should take that morality play for what it is: it may seem necessary at the time but it sure ends badly. Naysayers are a lot like scryers who complain that the proverbial crystal ball everyone else sees so clearly isn't *that* clear at all. What is it that George Eliot said? "Among all the forms of mistake," she wrote, "prophecy is the most gratuitous."[1] Shouldn't restraint be the order of the day, especially since so many naysayers have been wrong?

You'd think. But in the case of the Web, someone has to speak out, has to say aloud that the emperor doesn't have on any clothes. Too many people–especially many *intelligent* people–keep repeating that same inane bromide that libraries are obsolete, or are being made so by the Web, the Internet, the "Net."[2] This is particularly bedeviling, especially when so many *librarians* nod in agreement, but the library-is-dead-crowd is everywhere.

It's rare to open a professional library magazine and *not* find an article on why library search engines should be more like Google, or why the entire library shouldn't imitate the Web in some significant manner. For all other magazines, from business ones to ones on theology or the humanities, it's Google *über alles*. To hear the claque rehearse their lines, you'd think the Web had cured the common cold. I say enough already. Google will not replace anything, and the Web will not make libraries obsolete. Both are useful and important but neither is a panacea for anything, least of all *research*. Although this belief may place me in the company of the few, perhaps only the handful, it's company I prefer to keep.

Herewith are reasons why the Internet will not replace the library. But before going too far into that discussion, two disclaimers must be lodged. I have used the Web extensively since 1992, and even created Web pages when doing so required knowing elementary code. I have used the Web extensively to write the articles and books I've written, including this one. So my assertions about the Internet vis-à-vis the library do not qualify me as either a Luddite or a hypocrite.

The Luddite charge is one I know I cannot avoid but I'll make the case now that I know a fair amount about the Web and have used it enough to know both its merits *and its defects* (yes, there *are* some). I would never claim to be an expert on the Web, but as one who uses it daily, and has since its early, clunky inception, I know enough about it at least to know whereof I speak. I also know that we Americans love our technology almost as a much as we love our football (both have become ersatz spiritual obsessions). And, just like football, I know if you criticize technology you'll like be branded as an outcast, even a nutcase, for declaiming against the semi-official religion. Besides, wasn't the Unabomber one of the early critics of technology? Who wants to be thrown into that class!?

I, for one, don't, but someone must step forward to stop all this codswallop about the Web replacing libraries, or Google making them obsolete. Someone had to say something, so I did, first in an article and then a poster. But criticizing the Web is a dangerous area and one where I do not tread lightly. One respected librarian at a major research institution in the northeast saw my poster and wrote to tell me that the library "was nothing until the Web."[3] The assertion proved an astonishing one to me, especially when one considers that we've been without the Web for about 99.9% of our civilization! Alas, it's not the first such comment I've heard from colleagues. Anyway, the point is, I'm not a Luddite, though I'm pretty sure some who read this article will dismiss me after the first sentence as one because I dared criticize the God of Google or the Tao of Technology.

Although all those who criticize the Web are "straightway handled with a chain," not all of them should be. The coiner of the phrase, "paperless society," F. W. Lancaster, has come forward regretting saying that for many reasons, not the least of which is the one I contend with here: it has not made libraries obsolete.[4] Many doubts have now surfaced about the so-called social networking of MySpace.com and Facebook.com, which are discussed later. Thomas Friedman, author of the rightly famous *The World Is Flat*, now opines that he gets into a cab and he and the cabbies do not speak for miles, both of them multitasking like madmen.[5] Perhaps the world isn't really flat so much as we're just all flat-headed when it comes to the "wow" of the Web. Now comes word from the creator of the Web itself, not Al Gore, but the *real* inventor, Sir Timothy Berners-Lee, wondering aloud what HTML hath wrought.[6] Apparently, this grand experiment in democracy turns out to be a failed experiment in kakistocracy. So, perhaps I'm in pretty good company after all.

As for the hypocrite charge, it runs something like this. If you cite from the Web and use it, how can you criticize it? But I view this charge much as I would view a charge of a similar nature from one who, say, criticized traffic deaths and yet drove to work every day. Or take another example. Is a person who criticizes healthcare but holds health insurance and visits his physician annually a hypocrite? Would anyone be willing to call Hillary Clinton who held (and holds) possibly the best health insurance in the world as the First Lady (and now as a Senator) a hypocrite because she spearheaded a group to dismantle that healthcare while her husband served as President? Regardless of whether one thought her suggestions excellent, or just socialized medicine, I don't think one could say that because she used healthcare but also criticized it, she's hypocrite. Just because I cite Web-based articles here and elsewhere while claiming that it is a *most* inferior library-like substitute doesn't qualify me as a hypocrite either.

Okay then, so why is the Web no substitute for a library? Why do I level the charge that the Web is the new fool's gold?

Forget the Needle! Can You Just Tell Me Which Haystack?

We've all experienced Web-euphoria. You input a search term into Google (or Lycos, Hotbot, Yahoo) and get back 1,234,456,345 hits in 3.652 seconds. Wow! *That's* what I'm talking about! How can this *not* be better than a dumb old library where you have to think and actually look for your answers? Then you begin to scroll through the first ten hits, then the second ten, then the third ten and slowly your euphoria turns first to disappointment then to outright indignation. How dare the Web trick you like that!

All of this assumes you really look past the first ten hits. I teach search classes where I work and for the last seven years I've asked students (over 300 so far) how many go past the *first* screen. To date, only *one* has admitted to it, a nontraditional student over the age of forty. Now this is very anecdotal and unscientific, but also very descriptive. While the Web is great at supplying discrete data–Bogotá, 3.14, 5,280 feet–it isn't very good at providing you the *right bit of knowledge*. Because most search engines use relevancy ranking, the first ten or twenty or one hundred hits may or may not be what you want. Moreover, those same returns are not always the best: the Web is jammed-packed with misinformation, disinformation, fraud, and more.

Many examples abound. In 2002, the highly regarded Associated Press reported that PETA (People for the Ethical Treatment of Animals) had outfitted more than 400 deer in orange vests so hunters would mistake them for other hunters and not shoot them.[7] Guy Lockey, a sporting goods store owner offered a reward for each vested deer bagged. Although the story is just crazy enough to fit the usual PETA *modus operandi*, trapping a wild deer and fitting it with a vest is next to impossible. Moreover, Guy Lockey is a fictitious name. But if it came off the web, it had to be true, right?

Then there is the well-known but tragic one that occurred at Johns Hopkins and represents the limits of the Web, falling under the heading of what you don't know can hurt, perhaps even kill you. Ellen Roche, a seemingly healthy 24-year-old, volunteered for an asthma study at the well-known and highly regarded institute. After entering the study, she was given a drug protocol that had been vetted, or so it seemed, by the researchers. She inhaled a chemical treatment, hexamethonium, which led to the progressive failure of her lungs and her kidneys, and her eventual death.[8] This sad case is made all the more tragic because it could easily have been averted. The supervising physician, Dr. Alkis Togias, made what appeared to be a thorough search of the literature. He approved the drug as did the ethics panel who reviewed his research methodology. But Dr. Togias relied heavily on PubMed, an electronic source that only goes back to 1966. A traditional print search would have found articles published in the 1950s that warned against using this drug in such experiments for the very reason that Ms. Roche died: rapid, progressive lung and kidney failure. Togias relied on PubMed and even did a Google search on hexamethonium. But his search did not reveal the inherent danger with his drug protocol, though the warning existed in the citations section of *PoisonIndex Toxicologic Management.* These citations are on the Web but are not easily found by inexperienced searchers.

Because the Web is so easy to use as a publishing medium, because there is no gate-keeping, because there are no fact-checkers, misinformation is not only inevitable but also abundant. Some may argue that these misprisions are small and on balance unworthy of our attention. But in a less Web-based delivery of information, bad or incorrect information would never make it through all the hoops before being found as bogus. The Web's instant gratification attribute makes certain many bogus claims will be made public long before we learn that they are, in fact, specious.

Space does not allow a longer rehearsal of the millions of business scams, health frauds, and more. In the case of the latter, physicians are particularly worried because patients come into their offices having diagnosed their illness. These patients are hard to convince they are wrong. Of course there are excellent sites on the Web, such as WebMD, but there are also thousands of others that are not only wrong (such as the coughing-to-prevent-a-heart-attack), not only stupid, but also dangerous.

Weare18.com

We've always been a nation awash in pornography but now, because of the Web, we're drowning in an ocean of smut. In my own lifetime spanning barely a half century, pornography has gone from its once infamous brown paper wrappers to today's most revered and protected forms of "free speech." Sadly, the American Library Association (along with the usual suspects like the ACLU and First Amendment absolutists) have gone to great lengths to protect everyone's right to view any kind of intercourse with any kind of partner (human or not) anywhere. In its infancy, television did not hint at sexual misconduct (most *married* couples slept in *separate* beds) and mainstream movies had to pass the rigorous Hayes Commission standards. Today, gratuitous sex is rampant in mainstream movies, even when those R and NC-17 movies lose millions.[9] Meanwhile, television sitcom characters snigger about everything from veiled sexual innuendo to blatant declarations of every kind of sex known (and some unknown) to humankind. *Sub rosa* storylines, even in commercials, titter like junior high-schoolers over erectile dysfunction or vaginitis. Oh, we have come a long way, baby! Sex is everywhere.

So why pick on the Web? Is Web-based pornography really that big a deal? Are we a nation awash in voyeurism because the Web has made it so readily available? If statistics are any indication, it would appear a forgone conclusion. The argument here isn't that we have only recently discovered pornography. As almost any book or article is quick to point out, pornography has been around quite a long time. Livy records that certain Roman emperors spent their leisure hours viewing or reading it. Diogenes of Sinope, that quintessential liberal figure, fought against the customs of his day by eschewing manners, dressing shabbily and masturbating in public just to make a point.[10] The argument here isn't that pornography is new but that its nonstop ubiquity is courtesy of the Web.[11]

About 25% of all websites are pornographic, a seemingly small amount; but its influence is far-reaching. The Web boasts of nearly 400 million pornographic pages. Nearly a third of all *daily* searches (close to 70 million) are for pornographic retrievals. About 10% of all e-mails are pornographic (nearly 3 billion). Almost 40% of all downloads are pornographic in nature (nearly 2 billion), and close to 120,000 daily requests to Gnutella, a file-sharing network, are of the unquestionable constitutionally illegal child pornography kind. More than 100,000 sites on the Web are of children in pornographic repose.[12] KaZaA, another file-sharing network, has been downloaded more than two hundred million times, with more than four million users sharing and searching files at any given time, many of which are pornographic in content.[13] We are a nation that does not discriminate, either, as about three-fourths of all men and a quarter of all women admit to visiting pornographic websites regularly. Not to put too fine a point on it, more than 50% of all men who are members of the religious group "Promise Keepers" (and have pledged to stay away from such things) drink from the pornographic cesspool often.

So, is pornography a problem, and is it specifically a *Web* problem? To coin a phrase a former President once made famous, it depends on what how you define "problem." Among our *cahier de doleances* against the Web, pornography, and all its twisted sisters, ranks chief among them. While the Web did not invent pornography, it certainly made its longevity and ubiquity a certainty. Child predators have found a safe haven in the Web. Clearly the Web has made it more ubiquitous, more readily available, and far more likely to be part of *everyone's* Web existence, whether they like it or not.

This rich, supposedly unprecedented educational and information resource that will eventually replace libraries routinely delivers the worse that humankind can offer. It's important to remember, however, that pornography is not only available in millions of Web pages, but also in chat rooms, e-mails, alternative groups, FaceBook, MySpace, Friendster, and other so-called social communities. Moreover, the local child molester who might not have shown his face twenty years ago "shows" it in every community in America, thanks to the Web. The anonymity that the Web provides makes it easy to prey on the young and unsuspecting without the risk of capture, thus emboldening those who might otherwise not take the risk.[14] MySpace, especially, has become a haven for pedophiles and porn.[15]

In fact MySpace has become so bad ("skanky" as the *New York Times* puts it) that even corporate sponsors such as Weight Watchers and T-mobile have already pulled their ads or are threatening to do so. Some of these social community users are 14 years of age or even younger with such graphic profiles they cannot be repeated here. Some of the "more presentable" profiles include young girls "practicing to be porn stars" or the sharing of pictures of the anything-goes porn star Tera Patrick, and others. If you think pedophiles have missed this opportunity, think again. They are trolling for the wary and the not-so-wary.

The point is, the Web has made pornography ubiquitous. While the American Library Association opines against filters, it has yet to say one word about fellatio, cunnilingus and more that can be found on the Web by any eight-year old with Web access. A few years ago we shut down the apple juice industry because if one ate 70 alar-treated apples every day for 70 years, cancer *might* ensue. We shut down the apple juice industry "for the children." But the Web can produce both known and unknown sex acts in Technicolor and we all *defend* it as the newest and best library in the world. Readers need to remember that only fifteen years ago, *none* of this was available because the Web had not been invented yet. Moreover, *none* of this was available in *any* library. We are living proof of what one wag said: "As information doubles, knowledge halves and wisdom quarters."

Footnotes? Who Needs Them?

"You may observe," said Sir Arthur in Sir Walter Scott's *The Antiquary*, "that he never has any advantage of me in dispute, unless when he avails himself of a sort of pettifogging intimacy with dates, names, and trifling matters of fact–a tiresome and frivolous accuracy of memory, which is entirely owing to his mechanical descent."

"He must find it convenient in historical investigation, I should think, sir?" said the young lady.[16]

Ah yes, that "pettifogging intimacy with dates"! In our politically correct, let's-not-make-anyone-memorize-anything school of thought, those who are intimate with dates, names, facts and so on are constantly having to defend themselves against the modern-day know-nothings who wish everyone were as little informed as the least informed among us. The "snatch and grab" mentality of the Web encourages all of us to let *something* else do everything for you, including the thinking part. Part of our brave, new Web-world is to do everything in 3.25 seconds; we no longer have time for silly things like footnotes.

The Web, per se, is guilty of missing, omitting, or ignoring footnotes altogether. But this complaint is of a far more serious kind. While the dotcoms and the dotnets are certainly the most egregious offenders when it comes to vanishing footnotes, even the electronic proprietary databases–databases like *Lexis-Nexis, Academic Search Premier, Infoseek* and so on–offend insensibly and unnecessarily. Not only must librarians worry about the retention of electronic titles in aggregate databases, but also fret over whether to keep both print and electronic collections, for the sake of footnotes. Now, while wringing hands over what to do about lost titles within database collections, they now must also worry about a new phenomenon: linkrot.[17] Linkrot, or what some refer to as the half-life phenomenon, has become an increasing worry since the late nineties when it was first noticed. The Web had not been around long enough before then to notice the growing problem. Moreover, no one perhaps gave it any real thought.

In a study of some 416 citations over four years, researchers Bugeja and Dimitrova found that only 61% of them were still accessible.[18] Moreover, 19% contained an error in the URL while 63% did not cite the date they were accessed. This is an unprecedented turn of events, especially when one considers that only a decade and half ago such careless scholarship would have been unthinkable, not to mention unacceptable. While it is not a matter that is slipping by unnoticed, it is worse: it is slipping by with the full knowledge of many scholars.[19]

One might excuse it if the journals in question were what might be considered (it is silly to say it) in the academic world as "back-ups" or "second string" sources, assuming there is such a thing. But the sad state of affairs is that the journals in question are among the most prestigious in a specified discipline. Given that academe is a discipline wherein we teach others the importance of scholarly, honesty, and integrity, it is most odd to find that we, too, when pushed by the Web, simply accept the state of digital life in which we now find ourselves. We accept, like so many braying sheep, that this is the state of progressive affairs, and so we must learn to accept and adapt to it. Many already have. Baby-Boomers once chanted that no one would push them around; GenXers pride themselves on being independent, solitary. Yet when it comes to Web-based information, *both* groups take their marching orders from the Internet regardless of how inferior it may be.

But the linkrot story worsens. When researchers studied citations moving from .pdf to html formatting, a 17% failure was noted.[20] This means, at its simplest level, that not only it is likely that citations only four years old may not only not be on the Web at all (there is 39% chance they will be gone), but that common formatting changes will increase the likelihood of disappearing citations. What does this mean for Google's grand plans to digitize some 15 million volumes? Will these volumes (assuming–and this is a grand assumption–that Google can surmount the copyright challenges) be complete texts, or texts with vanishing footnotes? Yes, of course, these will be mere images of pages, or so we are assured. But is the mass digitization plan accounting for changes in the Web over time so that these materials are here year after year, decade after decade? Moreover, it is common knowledge (or at least it once was) that re-mastering of digitized texts must take place *at least* twice a decade.[21] If footnotes are vanishing, and original texts are lost or discarded, what about the future re-digitizing of these texts? Will it be possible to create a stable text, much less a definitive one? And while the subject of definitive texts is on the table for discussion, what about them? With this state of affairs can *any* digitized text be considered definitive?

Electronic law journals and medical journals are also coming to the foreground as linkrot-infested information resources. "Over the past decade," writes one researcher, "the use of Internet citations in the footnotes of law review articles has grown from a trickle to a flood. But it is well documented that Uniform Resource Locators (URLs) experience linkrot, that is, over time, the URL is more and more likely to become a dead link, making footnote citations worthless or nearly so."[22] In a discipline (law) where footnotes are, in large part, the "meat" of the article, this becomes much more a serious matter than just a handful of journals in an esoteric discipline. According to Lyons, there were four instances of Web citations in three law reviews in the early nineties. By 2003 there were more than 96,000.[23] This would not be a concern if these citations could be relied upon for a reasonable period of time but they cannot.

According to Lyons and others, within *one year*, almost 18% of Websites and nearly 32% of Webpages *had disappeared.* In one study cited by Lyons of 31 academic titles, almost half the links were dead at the end of a three-year period. In a study by *JAMA*, also cited by Lyons, of 515 scientific links, nearly 28% were useless after only twenty-four months.[24] What is perhaps most disconcerting is that law review journals have a standard–the *Bluebook* (Rule 18.2)–that specifically discourages the use of Internet-only citations. While proprietary databases do fare better, they are not immune to linkrot. This is because even proprietary databases like *Lexis-Nexis*, *InfoSeek*, and *Academic Source Premier* do not maintain the same core journals from year to year. Sometimes this occurs because publishers of those journals pull them. At other times, the vendor decides, for whatever reason, to replace a journal with another more frequently used and/or cited one. And so the linkrot saga continues, in law, in medicine, in academic and science journals.

Some will mock this as so much ado about nothing and will quote, approvingly, Noel Coward's assertion that looking up footnotes is like answering the doorbell while making love. While humorous, Coward's assertion is surely wrong for those who wish to substantiate a claim, or to look back at a claim to see from whence it came. Oddly, there was an Ophrah-sized hand-wringing over James Frey's fictional autobiography. Frey's book was eventually withdrawn. But let the Web sell you a pig in a poke and we all oink approvingly.

Google über alles

Google's grand plan to digitize 10+ million unique titles from the so-called G7: University of Michigan, Harvard University, Stanford University, Oxford University, the University of California, the University of Virginia, and the New York Public Library, seemed like a good, even a great idea. These 10+ million unique titles were most likely not being read regularly, few people had access to them, and no one had access to them all. What could possibly be wrong about it? When the news was announced in 2004, almost everyone jumped on board. The giant Google with its vast resources would undertake the project, the now G7 libraries (more by the time this article appears) would partner with Google, little read books would be showcased in those 100+ million daily hits, and everyone would be served. Or so we thought. Digital libraries do not appear all that difficult to build, do not require very many employees (easily the largest expenditure item in conventional libraries), and are, we are told, able to adapt quickly to market and technological demands. In the twilight of the new digital day, everything appeared possible. Then the radar screen began blipping with numerous intruders threatening to spoil our mad rush to the mass digitization party. But the trouble began even long before Google's plan. The symptoms were there, but few wanted to acknowledge them.

Like a frat party that begins well enough only to end in too much drinking, the next day hangovers ensued. Some began to question how all of this would be done. Others asked about copyright. The French asked why the titles Google chose to digitize were all English ones. A few librarians began thinking seriously about the implications of a giant Google library. Some scholars wondered about how Google would be reimbursed (would Hamlet's soliloquy appear alongside an advertisement for Viagra?). Not a few publishers asked why they were not consulted, and by late 2006, the Google plan began to flag.

It's not likely it will fall to half staff forever. Google has always prided itself on "built-in innovation" and so will surely find ways to make something on this order (though, perhaps, not of this magnitude) eventuate. Still, it brings to mind an important question: is the rush to mass digitization the right approach right now for scarce library dollars?

Obviously my answer is in the negative and here's why. We're rushing vast resources in this direction with no real standards, no real plans *other* than we will digitize these millions of books and then . . . what? We seem to think that once in cyberspace *everyone* will have them. But this is patently untrue. Only those will have them, assuming Google surmounts the copyright challenges, who also have high speed Internet access, a stable Internet Provider, good, regularly updated equipment, the ability to download, and unlimited free printing (where's a tree-hugger when you really need one?).[25]

We are nearly always given the scenario of the poor, underserved soul in the darkest of Dafur who will now have access to millions of titles. Really? Is this right before or right after he has died of malnutrition, scurvy, pox, and a million other hunger-deprived diseases? The fact of the matter is only in the U.S. could this be assumed, and even here, of, at most, only about 50% of the population. For example, the only way that I am able to navigate the Web with great ease is because I work for an institution that spends, literally, hundreds of thousands of dollars on access annually. If left to my own paltry pocketbook, I would not be accessing the Web every week, much less every hour of every day.

But let's assume that Google really is the new Guru when it comes to web-based information. What of those other tens of thousands of *lesser* (much lesser) digitization projects? Are those being held to high standards, are there funds for re-digitization, are they guilty of "cherry picking" their collections (picking the best and leaving the rest for the dustbin), and is anyone using digitization as a replacement for preservation? In the case of the latter, using digitization as a replacement for preservation, there is real concern. Digitization cannot, at least for now, *ever* be used as a substitute. Yet the problem remains that many are using it as such even though they know it's a bad replacement. Why? Because that's where the funding is. Years from now we'll know what Google et al. hath wrought in this mass hysteria but by then it may be too late to rectify any askance matters.

eBooks to the Rescue?

Surely eBooks will come to our rescue in this grand rush to all things Web-based. Sure, print books have been easy to handle, come in all shapes and sizes, can generally be carried everywhere and anywhere, but it's only a matter of time before eBooks replace them. Surely eBooks will prove all my assertions about the Web wrong!

The inevitability of eBooks is a safe bet because so much time, effort, and dollars have already been sunk into them although so little has been seen in return. eBooks have, in one shape or another, been in the reading conversation for more than 15 years.[26] In all that time, we are still far away from a consuetudinary acceptance of them. But their inevitability is secure because printed books are the new *bête noir*.[27]

eBooks are today *still* on the evolutionary chain's first link, at the point of the once two-shoebox-size mobile phone: clunky, cumbersome, frustrating, yet with some promise. What makes them less hopeful than mobile-phones-turned-ubiquitous-cell-phones is that they are not anywhere like an improvement over what they purport to replace. And therein lies the problem.

So far, all we have are *bad* imitations of print books, not grand improvements over an "outdated" medium. Formats are not interchangeable. eBook readers are not interchangeable and again, when one goes to invest, the initial start-ups are steep, beginning at about $400 and ending around $2,000. While the texts themselves may be cheaper than print counterparts (but not by much), there is still the problem of the reader.[28] But this is only the beginning. They also change the reading experience whether one reads them on a reader, or downloads an HTML text for reading on a computer. The argument is always that these changes enhance the reading experience. In fact, they radically change it.

For example, a text will be embedded with hyperlinks, colors, perhaps even a digital cicerone who guides the reader through the text. Whatever else one may say about these added electronic ingredients, they make the reading experience a *spectator* sport, not an intellectual encounter. The reader is led through the text; he/she does not read it. Rather than allowing the reader to think for himself/herself, the reader is led on a wild goose-chase to a myriad of other "helps" that serve only to exhaust (if they do not first confuse) the reader. Even if we suppose a strict e-text that precisely duplicates a printed text, the reader is still struggling through the new physiological experience of reading with a light in her eyes, not over her shoulder.[29] We may be able to "evolve" away from this process but it will not happen over the next 100 years. Even after 15 years, eBooks still only hold 5% of the reading population. Moreover, in Web-like "snatch and grab" fashion, "reading" is measured on eBooks in *minutes*, not in hours. So far we do not have anything approximating cover-to-cover reading. And yes, while this may change, surely after 15 years we might have something more than a whisper warehoused as a shout? When eBook users are not complaining about the readers, they are complaining about the lack of content.[30] Again, is this *really* a good way to use up very scarce library funds?

The Paperless Revolution Is Complete!

The din of grand claims about the Web often drowns out some of its inglorious failures. None is more colossal or more inglorious than the paperless society schlepped for the last thirty years as the coming brave, new world. In fact, everything about the Web, the Prime Mover of the paperless world, screams "Ultimate Significance" when we cannot possibly know that at this early stage. "The Internet is too young," writes Robert J. Samuelson, "for anyone to foretell its ultimate significance. . . . But some present claims aren't true."[31] Samuelson goes on to point out that it did *not* spread faster than any other innovation, that it *is* a work in progress, and that many other innovations have far outstripped it in seismic afterclap (take indoor plumbing, for example, or electricity). We forget that we are, as Robert Burton reminds us in the *Anatomy of Melancholy*, dwarves sitting on the shoulders of giants.[32] We moderns hate the thought that, not only did many things and many greater people come before us, but also that they invented many things far better than we have, including the Web.

Over the last twenty-five years, automation's prognosticators made increasingly bold claims abut the coming paperless age. Offices, businesses, industries, libraries, and universities would eventually all become paperless and the New Jerusalem would be ours at last. Some made claims by redefining the library as no longer a single entity but "a range of services" that would be (somehow) seamlessly connected and would reach beyond any one campus or laboratory.[33] Others suggested that the library would be freed, as if once a slave, from paper and occupy "infinite space" and be "interconnected in a transparent way."[34] (All predictions must apparently include either the word "seamless" or "transparent.") The library as a place would disappear; it would be replaced by a network of every imaginable file or database, there would be no walls, buildings would vanish, communities of every size would provide its citizens laptops, and electronic files would never, ever be lost.[35] Of course, there would *have* to be paradigm shifts for where would we be without them? Librarians and users would have to learn to accept those changeling paradigms or be lost in the dust of the parabolic arch, or some such matrix-like vacuum.

A funny thing happened on the way to the new paperless world: society didn't get the memo, maybe because it was e-mailed and ended up deleted as spam. Somewhere along the way the New Paperless Jerusalem ended in the pages of Samuel Butler's old *Erewhon*. The only paperless society so far successful occurs in the heady environment inhabited by George Jetson, his wife Jane, his daughter Judy, his son Elroy–well, you get the picture. The paperless society expired even before that new world began. We are no closer to the paperless world than we were thirty-five years ago when it was touted as the next new thing. Surely this helps explain why in the last ten years almost no one has been talking about it *but that has not stopped the forcible move in its direction.* What is disturbing to some is the continued march, lockstep really, toward this goal, although most, if not all the predictions of the coming paperless society ended early, or simply failed outright.

"We are drowning in information," writes John Naisbitt, "but starved for knowledge."[36] Naisbitt hits upon the very reason for this embarrassing failure. Along the way to paper-freedom, someone forgot to distinguish between an answer and the right answer, between information and the right information, between information (raw data), and knowledge (raw data turned into something usable). In other words, having an ocean of fish doesn't mean you've caught anything *yet*, and weltering in information does not mean you're awash in wisdom. Paper has allowed us to tame the *information* revolution that threatens to undo us. No one seemed to notice that having an industry–computers–that could churn out with lightning quick speed a disorganized morass of data did not mean we would be any better off than when we had to distill it into wisdom as we once slowly ferreted it out on paper. Take, for example, the new datum that 75% of all e-mails today are spam.[37] In the end, this grand new educational resource that's better than libraries threatens to undo us with "You May Be A Winner!" notices.

Why does so much of the world remain agog over the putative but little seen "vast" resources of the Web? Sure, eight billion pages (the web's current size) is vast. But when two-thirds or more are the equivalent of a crank phone call, "vast" suddenly seems small. Yet in our rush to make everything electronic, we are called upon to ignore most of these crank phone calls and stand amazed in the presence of emoticons, video clips of stupid animal tricks, Internet Solitaire, a cesspool of pornography–and all for the grand benefit of getting tomorrow's weather forecast today, or being able to e-mail the latest puns to your best friend . . . who happens to work down the hall. But such talk will only land us in the Office of Luddite Control. We must face up to the fact that the paperless society is winning even when it's losing. Sadly, many of its wins come largely from those in my own profession, librarianship.

The modern version of this "treason of the clerks" goes like this. Recently OCLC, the national database of library-owned materials, released a report that proves the treasonous clerks are not only winning battles, they may have already won the war.[38] Not all the news is inexorably bad. Students are using libraries, have library cards, and have used a library Web site.[39] But students go on to point out that library usage in the future will remain flat, that the Web is out-vying libraries for "information," and that search engines are the preferred (first and last) approach to research.[40] Moreover, almost 70% are more likely to begin (and, sadly end) with Google, regardless of the fact that vast sums of money are being spent by libraries on proprietary databases chock full of scholarly research.[41] The *first* choice of students (*college* students, mind you) is a search engine (Google, Yahoo, Ask.com, MSN Search, etc.)–72%–over a physical library (14%). In other words, they are choosing free search engines over multimillion dollar libraries five times as often.[42]

Some may be shaking their heads ruefully at this point. Poor fellow, the information highway built its right-of-way to zoom past his epigone library. He didn't adapt his "business" to the growing demands of the electronic world and his customers are leaving him.[43] This charge would resonate more loudly if the inventor of the phase, "the paperless society," F. W. Lancaster, were not himself having second thoughts.[44] Lancaster recalls when he coined the phrase at a conference in Finland as describing "a largely paperless, network-based communications system having many of the characteristics to today's Internet-based environment."[45] He saw the confluence of events moving us quickly along to a time when most everything would grow out of this putative electronic medium. "As the transition actually occurred, however, I became less enthusiastic about the developments and implications and, in the past few years, *downright hostile to them.*"[46]

Lancaster cites dehumanization as much to blame, arguing that, at least in the United States, it has replaced the human element. But he goes on to blame librarians because they have become "completely uncritical of information technologies."[47] While this is largely true, it cannot be left unsaid that those of us who have been critical have been branded as Luddites or worse.[48] He also goes on to point out "wild assertions" about technology that cannot possibly be true, such as providing access to information anywhere, any time, any place, because they assume if it is in a database, it can be found easily, when "nothing could be further from the truth."[49] He argues that many scholars and experienced researchers are happy with results found *until they discovered how many important items they missed* (Individual librarians, as well as a team of librarians, missed fewer important citations but more than they should have.).

If we proceed along these lines, searching for materials to answer pertinent questions of inquiry will be all too painfully familiar: "Press one, if your answer is yes; press two, if you need more help. Press three, if . . ." After a long line of such questions the poor user will be referred back to the menu, and the endless, useless loop will begin anew. And for what? For the paperless chase that leads to nowhere.

A Mile Wide and a Mind-Numbing Inch Deep

Throughout this article we have examined the hidden costs of the Web, such as its very content, or the lack thereof, and dispelled many myths regarding the size of the Web. We also addressed issues such as fraud, pornography, scams, hate sites, identity theft, and the vast numbers of young people providing TMI–too much information–about themselves and others in places like MySpace.com and Facebook.com, without respect to future consequences (when did a library ever do this to anyone, much less to young people?). While we have been quick to point out that anyone of these obvious or hidden costs would hardly be enough by themselves to question the Web's utility, cumulatively they do present a strong argument against the Web's stance as a possible substitute for a full-service library.

Reading comprehension now presents itself as a possible casualty of the Web.[50] We know for example that when we read on the Web we do not read in detail but in snatches (sometimes referred to as the "snatch and grab" process) and not in the same manner as we read printed books, cover-to-cover. Yet very few are examining this problem in great detail with an eye to possible contraindications. Even so, preliminary studies do not provide promising results for the future. Indeed, if anything, they point to just the opposite, that Web-based "reading" contributes to an even more cursory reading comprehension, along with a decline in literacy. Very little is being done to point out how this problem is a negative consequence of making all our access to information digital. As with most of the problems we have encountered in connection to the Web, our solution appears to be that we need more of the Web, not less; and if it turns out to be a bad thing, well, it will somehow manage to right itself in the long run.

Reading proficiency scores for students have been declining for a number of years, and dramatically since 1990.[51] For example, reading proficiency for 9 year olds from 1971 to 1999 has remained almost static, rising from 208 to 212 (scores that are just above the barely literate rates) and then dropping only slightly and leveling off entirely. The 212 level, the highest one reached, is barely above the "partial skills and understanding" level, and far removed from "learns from specialized reading materials," a level we hope they will achieve before entering college. Although the National Assessment of Educational Progress (NEAP) has been conducting reading studies for a number of years, some would argue that the proficiency levels noted there (in the low 200s) may not even rise to the level of what many would call literate.

While these students may well be able to read, they still exhibit what is sometimes referred to as a "knowledge deficit." Such young people are unlikely to overcome this lost or weak ability once it is entrenched at the age of 9, the last age at which any positive gains in reading can be measured. It could be argued that the stagnant levels of this proficiency roughly correspond to the rise of computers in the home and in the school as merely coincidental, but it strikes some as more than that. If the skills are weak to begin with, and activities and interests pull readers possessing those weak skills into yet other reading proficiency-attenua-

ting activities, strengthening those reading skills later will be highly unlikely.[52]

In *more than twenty years*, the skill could not be improved, even mar-
ginally (a period, it should be pointed out that mimics the rise of the
computer age). It appears as if literacy simply stopped growing. Furthermore, while the levels increase somewhat at age 13 (in the middle
250s, barely a literate reading ability), at age 17 those skills remain too
weak to understand complicated information. Again, reading levels at
each age do not improve so that the level of reading proficiency at ages
13 and 17 in students in 1971 was equal to those measured in students
more than twenty years later, in 1999. In other words, today's students
are no better in spite of all the money, time, energy, and programs (online and otherwise) we have applied to reading improvement.[53]

Reading proficiency should at least require at a minimum some basic
literacy, something these figures do *not* show. In fact, by 2009 students
in grades 4, 8, and 12 must be able "to read both literary (fiction, nonfic-
tion, and poetry) and information texts (exposition, argumentation, per-
suasive and procedural texts or documents)" in order to declare one
reading with proficiency.[54] Current scores indicate that we are light years
from achieving that goal. Why would we add *anything* to the mix that
weakens our chances of getting there?

In other words, the abysmal scores previously reported will only grow
worse as standards tighten. The 2009 NEAP standards define reading
as "an active and complex process that involves understanding written
text; developing and interpreting meaning; and using meaning as appropriate to type of text, purpose and situation."[55] If students are encouraged
to "snatch and grab," if they are losing vocabulary, if they are rapidly declining in reading interests the older they get (and they are), the Web
should be the last place we focus their attention. It behooves us all the
more to make certain we are not saddling students with a skill acquisition
(the digital context) that will only deepen the pool of potential illiterates.
The Web has us on a fast-track collision course with shared ignorance. It
encourages *spectators* to knowledge, not active participants. Students
view watching television or a computer screen as equivalent activities.

Moreover, online material has also increased plagiarism to epidemic
proportions.[56] Having more of the same will be unlikely to decrease these
offenses. Moreover, today's students do no read these texts, but merely
snatch and grab what they want, not the best of scholarly practices or a
way to improve reading proficiency. Having millions more books to pil-
fer does not seem like the best way of attenuating our current and growing illiteracy problem. It is not that students today are so much less

virtuous than students of former years, but that having such an arsenal at one's fingertips only encourages more snatching and grabbing, more reading in bits and pieces, and more cutting and pasting. It is too risible to think that students will read these texts online from digital-cover-to-digital-cover when all evidence to date indicates they are spending *minutes* with online books, not hours. We believe that students *must* be learning better because the "text" in question not only has words, but also has pictures, sounds, video clips, and more. We think that because students are forced to numerous other important and tangential concerns, the learning experience is thereby deeper and made more powerful. What we do not have to support these velleities are empirical data substantiating that these are transferable skills. We just assume it *must* be so, and that wishing will make it right. Even when we know that "many Web-based environments also introduce a new set of cognitive barriers *that can cause competent readers of conventional text to be cognitively overloaded and frustrated*, we damn those torpedoes and fund another round of mass digitization projects.[57]

Furthermore, a new study now indicates students cannot multitask. While they may well be "ultra-communicators," they cannot read, study, use the cell phone, text message, and listen to their iPods at the same time, though most try. We also know that they are rapidly growing allergic to text-based materials. This *should* alarm us. Whether we like it or not, literacy is still measured largely by the written (i.e., printed) word.[58] It does not seem either right or wise that we should encourage students to become independent of text-based learning. Moreover, we should make absolutely certain that any Web-based learning is equivalent to text-based learning before we send a generation of students to their academic peril. It's no secret that elementary children are fascinated by what they see on the Web, especially if pictures, video, and audio clips are present. But if these readers become too distracted by the technology, are they still learning?

The so-called transferable skills do not appear to be as transferable as we once thought. Web-based learning not only proves to be more difficult, but also capturing all the right elements–hardware, software, analysis of contents and so on–is very elusive. Even on college campuses we find that a variety of approaches meant to meet the so-called various kinds of learning are just as likely to be as bad as it is good. For every young person who feels emboldened to speak up in the anonymous context of Web-based or online environments, a dozen more are frustrated or annoyed by it. This should not come as any surprise to those who have tried to force audiovisual learning into the classroom. While it does not impede learning per se, many have found regardless of the approach used that such "teachable moments" turn quickly into disruptive ones and class management imbroglios.

We are progressing too rapidly down a descent from which we may never recover. When young people are poorly educated, they spend a lifetime regretting it. So, too, does the society which allows it to happen. As the "can-do" nation, we are slow to admit defeat about any invention but especially about one that appears as successful to us as the Web. However, we cannot turn a blind eye to its defects. Mary Shelly's *Frankenstein* began innocently enough. We need not let our modern-day Frankenstein, the Web, end with the same fate as hers. Now comes the news that many students are using the same moral code in instant messaging that they use in formal research papers and cannot understand why it's unacceptable.

Finally, there is the Web content itself. No matter what one chooses to look at, what the Web proffers does not inspire us with its educational content. Whether one chooses the "best" of the Web from Yahoo! Google, or even Web-savvy experts, what young people and old rate as the best is far from the true educational content that even a small library proffers. For example, in October 2006, Google purchased YouTube, a site offering thousands of videos. Before the purchase, YouTube could boast hundreds of thousands of hits, apparently the *only* measure of a "good" Website. Today, the issue of copyright emerges again and threatens to constrain the site. Already numerous clips available in one month are the next month or the month after removed.

In the fall of 2006, I looked at the top 100 videos. The headers proved amusing, showing everything from "Young girl with large hooters" to a young man trying to set fire to his flatulence with a cigarette lighter, to some white guy trying to dance. *This* is the new educational site that threatens libraries?

Of course there are valuable videos on this site (though not much I could find in the top 100 that one would want to spend much time examining). When this site is coupled with the fact hat 75% of e-mails are now spam, perhaps all our "work" on the Web is so much wheel-spinning. Sure, for *advertisers* seeking to reach millions of people, the Web is a bonanza. But should this be the work of a library? In November 2006, I heard a presentation at a library conference about Google Print. During the question and answer period, one participant in the audience asked about Google's plan to make money off all this. The representative said that Google "was not yet sure how they were going to *mone-*

tize all this" but perhaps it might be something like the ads that appear so familiar now. Or, perhaps worse, the full text will be pay-per-view?

And this is just what troubles me and others. I'm certain I do not want Dante with an ad for Virago, or one for erectile dysfunction. Or even for clothes or anything in between. There may still be time to make the Web what it should be, a tool, like many other tools, that can aid and abet our pursuit of turning information into knowledge, and that knowledge into wisdom. But the present state of affairs puts us exactly light years from this goal. Are librarians paying any attention to these things? Is anyone? A few more years down this road and the question will no longer matter. We will have, not the future we want, but the future we allowed. We have arrived on the Information Superhighway, all right, but are we rushing all too fast to make libraries, and library services, that highway's first roadkill?

NOTES

1. George Eliot. *Middlemarch* 1950 ed., London: Zodiac Press, 83.

2. Yes, yes, I know that the Web and the Internet are not synonymous terms though they have become so in common parlance. Rather that try to swim upstream entirely by keeping the two separate, I have chosen to use them interchangeably. The Internet is, of course, made up of protocols or rules that let computers "talk" to each other. The Web or the World Wide Web, on the other hand, is made up of software protocols that run on top of the Internet and that let users see and access files stored on other computers. For more on this see Chris Sherman and Gary Price. *The Invisible Web: Uncovering Information Sources Search Engines Can't See.* CyberAge Books., Medford, New Jersey, 2001, specifically their chapter 1. I also use Google as eponymous for the Web.

3. For the poster, see <www.winthrop.edu/dacus> and click on the "ten reasons link." All the proceeds go to the library's faculty development fund. Look on the bright side. If you disagree, buy a poster anyway and suggest that your dean go to a few technology conferences.

4. F. Wilfrid Lancaster. "Second Thoughts on the Paperless Society." *Library Journal* (September 15, 1999) Vol. 124 (15), 48. See also his "The Paperless Society Revisited." *American Libraries* (September 1985) Vol. 16 (8), 553-555.

5. Friedman, Thomas L. "The Taxi Driver." *New York Times* (Wednesday, November 1, 2006) LE, A23.

6. Ghosh, Pallab. (November 02, 2006) "Web inventor Fears for the Future." BBC News accessed via <http://news.bbc.co.uk/go/pr/fr/-/1/hi/technology/6108578.stm> on November 7, 2006.

7. Paul S. Piper. "Web Hoaxes, Counterfeit Sites, and Other Spurious Information on the Internet." In *Web of Deception: Misinformation on the Internet.* Anne P. Mintz, ed. Medford, NJ: CyberAge Books, 2002, 7-8. Fox News also reported the story in January 2002.

8. Eva Perkins. "Johns Hopkins's Tragedy: Could Librarians Have Prevented a Death?" *Information Today, Inc.* (August 7, 2001). Accessed via http: <www.infotoday.com/newsbreaks/nb010806-1.htm>, March 2006. The description which follows comes from this article. See also Susan Levine. "Hopkins Researcher Faulted in Death." *The Washington Post* (July 17, 2001) accessed via *Lexis-Nexis* February 2006.

9. Movie critic Michael Medved has discussed this oddity. G-rated movies do two and three times better at the box office than PG, PG-13, R, or NC-17 movies. Yet producers make five or even six times as many of the PG, PG-13, R, and NC-17 movies than the G-rated ones that earn so much more money.

10. The story is repeated in Siva Vaidhyanathan. *The Anarchist in the Library: How the Clash Between Freedom and Control Is Hacking the Real World and Crashing the System.* New York, Basic Books, 2004, 25.

11. Some of the best books for discussing the philosophical underpinnings of pornography and its deleterious effects on all of society are as follows: Robert P. George. *The Clash of Orthodoxies: Law, Religion, and Morality in Crisis.* Wilmington, Del.: ISI Books, 2001; Pamela Paul. *Pornified: How Pornography Is Transforming Our Lives, Our Relationships, and Our Families.* New York: Times Books, 2005; Roger Shattuck. *Forbidden Knowledge: From Prometheus to Pornography.* San Diego: Harcourt Brace, 1997; United States House of Representatives. Committee on Energy and Commerce. Subcommittee on Commerce Trade, and Consumer Protection. *Online Pornography: Closing the Door on Pervasive Smut: Hearing Before the Subcommittee on Commerce, Trade, and Consumer Protection of the Committee on Energy and Commerce,* House of Representatives, One Hundred Eight Congress, Second Session. May 6, 2004. Washington: U.S. Government Printing Office, 2004. Paul's book is good because Paul is herself a First Amendment die-hard and *Times* reporter. Shattuck's thesis is that there are things that we can do that we should not and no better example exists than the widespread availably of pornography. That is, just because we *can* do something doesn't mean we *should.*

12. Other sources indicate that in 2005, almost 75% of searches worldwide were for pornographic material.

13. House of Representatives. *Stumbling onto Smut: The Alarming Ease of Access to Pornography on Peer-to-Peer Networks: Hearing Before the Committee on Government Reform.* House of Representatives, 108th Congress, March 13, 2003, 1. KaZaA and Gnutella are two of many file sharing sites. Others include Morpheus, BearShare, and Grokster.

14. Dick Thornburgh and Herbert S. Lin, eds. *Youth, Pornography and the Internet.* National Academy Press, Washington, DC, 2002, ES-3.

15. Rebecca Hagelin. "Porn, Pedophiles, Our Kids and MySpace." Townhall.com. Available at <ww.townhall.com/opinion/columns/rebeccahagelin/2006/05/30/199114.html>. Accessed June 2006.

16. Sir Walter Scott. *The Antiquary*, New York: Macmillan & Co., 1895, 43.

17. For the so-called hybrid collections, see Mark Rowse. "The Hybrid Environment: Electronic-Only versus Print Retention." *Against the Grain* (April 2003), 24-28. The problem of lost titles is this: an aggregate database can contain 100 titles in September and 100 in May. The trouble is they are not always the *same* 100 titles. Many libraries come to know about these lost or vanishing titles only after patrons come to them complaining that what they saw last month isn't there this month. For more,

see the book, *Fool's Gold: Why the Internet Is No Substitute for a Library*. McFarland, 2007.

18. Michael Bugeja and Daniela V. Dimitrova. "The Half-Life Phenomenon: Eroding Citations in Journals." *The Serials Librarian* Vol. 49 (3), 117.

19. Scott Carlson. "Scholars Note the Decay of Citation to Online References." *The Chronicle of Higher Education*. (March 18, 2005), A30. Also cited in Bujega and Dimitrova.

20. Bugeja and Dimitrova, 121-122.

21. Some experts claim re-mastering is required every *three* years.

22. Susan Lyons. "Persistent Identification of Electronic Documents and the Future of Footnotes." *Law Library Journal* (Fall 2005) Vol. 97 (4), 681. Accessed via Lexis-Nexis, viewed, May 2006.

23. Ibid., 681.

24. Ibid., 683.

25. No one but no one reads anything on the Web after the third screen, and this is being generous!

26. To be honest, eBooks have been promised for the last *fifty* years. See Jennifer Adamec. "EBooks in the College Classroom." Unpublished Thesis. N.p.: MS Publishing, 2006, 2.

27. See Scott Carlson. "Library Renovation Leads to Soul Searching at Cal Poly." *Chronicle of Higher Education* (September 1, 2006) Vol. LIII (2), A59-61, where professors and librarians complain about the shift from print to online exclusively, and where print is considered so passé.

28. In some cases, readers are charged for books that are in public domain. While the charge may only be a nominal one (say $3 or $4), one still must pay for what is freely available elsewhere on the Web. This fee is ostensibly to defray the cost for loading in the Sony Connect eBook Reader format.

29. Bear in mind that we have been reading with the light (whether candle or electric) over our shoulders for the last 500 or so years.

30. Content is pre-chosen so one is electing what *someone* else thinks one should read, not what *you*, the reader, have decided to read. Some critics will complain that lack of choice is always the case in any library one enters. Perhaps, but I like my odds in a library of half a million books over one with only 5,000 choices, most of which are the usual half-baked best-sellers.

31. Robert J. Samuelson. *Untruth: Why Conventional Wisdom Is (Almost Always) Wrong*. AtRandom.com: New York, 2001, 218.

32. My favorite edition is the Vintage, published in 1977, a reprint of the 1932 Everyman edition. The book was of course published in 1621 and is a towering monument to scholarship of the highest, best, and most humorous kind, though not many critics see the latter. I cannot help but point out he, in addition to spending a lifetime on this magnificent book, was also a college librarian.

33. Mark Kirby and Nancy H. Evans. "The Network Is the Library." *EDUCOM Review* (Fall 1989) Vol. 24 (3), 16. Also quoted in Karen M. Drabenstott. *Analytical Review of the Library of the Future*. Council on Library Resources, Washington, 1994, 9.

34. Landoni Monica, Nadia Catenazzi and Forbes Gibb. "Hyper-Books and Visual-Books in an Electronic Library." *Electronic Library* (June 1993) Vol. 11 (3), 176. Also quoted in Karen M. Drabenstott. *Analytical Review of the Library of the Future*. Council on Library Resources, Washington, 1994, 10.

35. Karen M. Drabenstott. *Analytical Review of the Library of the Future*. Council on Library Resources, Washington, 1994, 11, 15, 20, 27.

36. Also quoted in Walt Crawford and Michael Gorman. *Future Libraries: Dreams, Madness, & Reality*. Chicago: American Library Association, 1995, 4.

37. "Ipswich, Inc., Warns that Spam Continues to Rise." Accessed via <http://www.ipswitch.com/company/press_releases/060831_spamometer.asp>, (August 31, 2006) viewed September 2006.

38. OCLC Online Computer Library Center. *College Students' Perceptions of Libraries and Information Resources*. OCLC Online Computer Library Center: Dublin, Ohio, 2006. This is a companion piece to an earlier report mentioned in this book, *Perceptions of Libraries and Information Resources*, 2005.

39. Ibid., 1-1.

40. Ibid., 1-2, 1-4, 1-7.

41. Ibid., 1-8.

42. Ibid., 1-11.

43. I should add that while I cannot extrapolate for all libraries, the one where I work has increased in usage over the last seven years as measured by our door counts.

44. F. Wilfrid Lancaster. "Second Thoughts on the Paperless Society." *Library Journal* (September 15, 1999) Vol. 124 (15), 48. See also his "The Paperless Society Revisited." *American Libraries* (September 1985) Vol. 16 (8), 553-555.

45. Ibid.

46. Ibid. (Emphases mine.)

47. Ibid.

48. I would not want to suggest his comment here *contra* electronic everything is the only reason, or even a primary one, that Lancaster himself has had troubles of late, but the timing is surely right. Only recently he had to step down as the editor of *Library Trends*, a move that was not only not of his making, but also not of his liking. It strikes me that the "trends" portion of that journal's name may well not like the idea that its editor is not fully on board with the current electronic *uber alles trend*? See "Lancaster Steps Down from *Library Trends* but Not by Choice." *Library Hotline* (August 14, 2006), 3.

49. Lancaster, 49.

50. I am not the first to raise this issue. See Sven Birkerts. *The Gutenberg Elegies: The Fate of Reading in an Electronic Age*. Boston: Faber and Faber, 1994. Birkerts' book was prophetic, foreseeing more than a decade before it happened most of what I record here.

51. Figures for what follows have come from *Trends in the Well-Being of America's Children*, 2003, specifically "Achievement/Proficiency." See also Tom Loveless. *How Well Are American Students Learning?* The 2006 Brown Center Report on American Education. Washington: The Brooking Institution, 2006, 8-11.

52. It isn't part of this argument about libraries and literacy but it is interesting to note that the Brown Report also points out that not only do students not do better if they are happy (i.e., have strong self esteem), but that trying to making learning relevant not only does not improve student learning but may also very well impede it. See Tom Loveless. *How Well Aare American Students Learning?* The 2006 Brown Center Report on American Education Washington: The Brooking Institution, 2006, 13-18.

53. Loveless, 327-330.

54. National Accessible Reading Assessment Projects. *Defining Reading Proficiency for Accessible Large-Scale Assessments: Some Guiding Principles*. February

17, 2006. Minneapolis, MN, 1. Available at <www.narap.info>. Viewed, September, 2006. 3. The changes are in response to standards made tighter by the NCLB Act. While flexibility is stressed, it is flexibility not in what defines proficiency but in what a child is able to read.

55. Ibid., 6.

56. Center for Academic Integrity, at <http://www.academicintegrity.org/>.

57. Julie Coiro. "Reading Comprehension on the Internet: Expanding Our Understanding of Reading Comprehension to Encompass New Literacies." *Reading Teacher* (February 2003) Vol. 56 (5) 462.

58. Robin Goodfellow. "Online Literacies and Learning: Operational, Cultural and Critical Dimensions." *Language and Education* (2004) Vol. 18 (5), 380. While some of what Goodfellow argues here agrees with my conclusions, he, too, is more hopeful about the future of Web-based learning than am I.

Who Holds the Keys
to the Web for Libraries?

Emily F. Blankenship

INTRODUCTION

The vast majority of knowledge now lies outside the realm of a physical library. The general public and many librarians now rely upon mega search engines to locate, in a timely manner, the most obscure data. Libraries could still play vital roles in these transactions because libraries can provide access to more scholarly resources, but the mega search engines, in reality, serve as Internet guideposts for most people and our challenge is to bring people back to their library holdings and services.

To paraphrase Dr. Vartan Gregorian during his speech at the American Library Association Annual Conference in June 2007, "Librarians are functionaries of our society. They have not changed the course of library service, but they have been changed by outside powers."[1] Google, Yahoo!, and Microsoft comprise the top three powers or mega search engines that are slowly and systematically changing the face of reference work. Librarians must use their advanced search skills in partnership with Google, Yahoo!, and Microsoft in order to provide timely, high quality, and relevant reference work to the new generation of users.

BACKGROUND

Seemingly just a few years ago, communities turned to the knowledgeable reference librarian who could place his/her finger on the correct page of information. Then, in 1996, came the wake-up call found within the Benton Foundation's report "Buildings, Books and Bytes: Libraries and Communities in the Digital Age." Benton's report focused on frequent library users and their perception of the library of the future.

The youngest Americans polled, those between the ages of 18 and 24, were found to be the least enthusiastic boosters of maintaining and building library buildings. This age group, commonly known as Generation Y, was also the least enthusiastic of any age group about the importance of libraries in a digital future. The young poll participants voted to spend their money on personal computer systems rather than contribute the same amount in tax dollars to the library. When asked to think about the role of libraries in the future, they placed libraries firmly in the past. "In 30 years," the Generation Y group noted, libraries would be relegated to a "kind of museum where people can go and look up stuff from way back when."[2]

The library of the future, according to the young Benton Foundation poll participants, far from being a technology leader, would function as an historical archive. The young participants presented an equally diminished view of the future role of librarians. The participants noted that librarians could perform a useful role as navigators in the as-yet difficult-to-navigate universe of the Internet. Yet, poll participants just as easily sanctioned the notion that trained library professionals could be replaced with community volunteers, such as retirees. For these unsophisticated library users, the concept of "librarians as trained professionals" was nebulous at best.[3]

Predictions from the Benton Foundation report proved to be on track. From 1997 to 2007, the public perception of the need for actual reference librarian work changed so much that the relevancy of the existence of libraries and reference desks is now questioned. The concept of a reference search, itself, has been transformed in the popular mind from perusing printed multivolume sets of works and printed serials indexes to an Internet search and the mania with all things Internet. Reference librarians are continuing to find increasing competition from the massive growth of the mega search engines like Google, Yahoo!, and MSN Search. Google, with its academic search engine, Google Scholar, provides especially alarming search statistics, competition, and annoyance to conventionally trained reference librarians.

TRADITIONAL REFERENCE SERVICES
FACE COMPETITION

Maurice York, in his recent article regarding Google Scholar, notes that librarians are divided into two camps regarding the use of Google Scholar: the purists, those who wish to protect their users from the gap-ridden, non-scholarly content; and those who are in some way trying to come to terms with the new 800-pound gorilla in their living room by introducing it to users in a cautious manner.[4]

Librarians possess legitimate concerns about users embracing acceptance of the mega search engines. Shared is the central fear that users will abandon expensive library databases and the library catalog and proceed to use the mega search engines exclusively for their research.

Support for reference librarian concern is shown in the results from East Carolina University's 2007 LibQUAL+ survey. Of the respondents, 58.23% said they used non-library gateways daily to retrieve information; 12.85% of the respondents stated they accessed library resources through the library gateway daily. Finally, only 2.81% of the respondents reported actually using resources housed on the library premises on a daily basis.[5]

Nancy Becker, in her article "Google in Perspective: Understanding and Enhancing Student Search Skills" notes that during a study of undergraduate student search behavior, "many college students continue to assign unwarranted primacy and authority to information found through Google and on the Web."[6] Ms. Becker further states that many of the students were able to articulate the importance of source evaluation for assessing the authority and reliability of Web-based resources. In practice, however, the same students usually abandoned source evaluation and followed the path of least resistance, relying exclusively on basic Google searching. Librarians now share the experience of being relegated to the brink of irrelevancy. Librarians are daily encountering users eliciting exclamations such as "I have looked all over the Internet for articles, but didn't find any. Now I'll ask you!"

Recently, the Search Engine Users report issued by the Pew Internet & Life Project found that most Internet users were naïve about doing research via the Internet. Overall, 18% of searchers said they could consistently distinguish between paid and unpaid search results and 70% of the searchers stated they were comfortable with the concept of paid or sponsored results.[7] This finding is particularly ironic, as nearly 50% of the users stated they would stop using search engines if they thought engines were not clearly designating paid results. Such outcomes demonstrate that search engine users are unaware of the analogous sets of content commonly presented by search engines.

PROSPECTIVE PATRONS AND NEW EXPECTATIONS

In the summer of 2004, the Pew Internet & American Life Project released its report on American Internet use. The Pew findings answer the very important question: "Who searches the Internet?" The answer is nearly everyone. According to Pew, 84% of adult Internet users, about 108 million United States citizens, have used search engines to help them find information on the Web.[8] Only the use of e-mail, with approximately 120 million users, eclipses searching in popularity as an Internet activity. The amazing part, at the core of these phenomena, is one person in front of a screen, typing in a query. Prospective library users, now also known as searchers, expect the mega search engines to bring back perfect results within seconds.

People want results now, and they desire perfect answers without learning an unwieldy programming language or drilling through copious layers of Web pages on an academic library Web site to reach the desired article. As the Benton Foundation report summarizes, the existence of the Internet, home computers, super-bookstores, and private information brokers require libraries, of all types, to change their means of providing the materials the users want and need.[9] Richard Wayne, writing about technology trends in Texas libraries notes, "Google has become the bane of many librarians and library school professors. Yet, the public–and even many librarians–love Google, and Google continues to grow like gangbusters."[10] People have become accustomed to almost instantaneous answers; now it is up to librarians to adopt new technologies and means of providing reference services or to face extinction.

In further evidence of the changing tide of librarian opinion, Jan Lewis, Associate Director for Library Services at East Carolina University, notes:

> It is clear that most of the world, including our students, are "Googling." Google Scholar looks and works like the Google they are familiar with, yet gets them to the content of some (not nearly all) of our licensed scholarly content materials that they would not otherwise be able to access through Internet search engines. We want to enable access to our licensed resources however we can to maximize use by our students. We hope that once they get into a database at the article level through a Google Scholar search, they may decide to use the database's search functions for more in-depth information retrieval.[11]

THE COMPETITION IN NUMBERS

Where are the students and general populous finding the answers to their questions while searching on the Internet? Many answers are found in the 2007 Piper Jaffray Research Report entitled *The User Revolution.* Released in February 2007, the Piper Jaffray Research Report states:

> Google dominates the United States search market with 46.3% of users performing their searches via Google. Yahoo! is a distant second with 28.5% of the United States search market share. MSN-Microsoft appears in third place with 10.5%, Ask follows with 5.4%, AOL holds 4.9%. Various other search engines comprise the remaining 3.4% of the United States search market. Piper Jaffray expects Google to continue to make gains in the volume of searches until leveling off at around 70% of the total search volume.[12]

Frighteningly for some librarians, John Battelle, founder and chairman of Federated Media Publishing notes, "the search engine of the future isn't really a search engine as we know it. It's more like an intelligent agent–or as Larry Page told me, a reference librarian with a complete mastery of the entire corpus of human knowledge."[13] Libraries indeed may soon be in peril if they continue to lag behind in adoption of new technology. Such lag causes the public to assume that libraries are old-fashioned. In stark contrast, the mega search engines are issuing press releases for each minuscule update or change.

Larry Page has not missed a step in his path to knowledge domination, yet. Google comes to us offering harmony, but on its own terms, which libraries have not attempted to challenge or even question. The challenge we face is one of understanding both the existing power and the potential of such a world knowledge force. As Google moves into for-fee services, libraries must work out the business models which suit our positions and discontinue being functionaries.

In June 2007, searchers in the United States conducted 8.0 billion searches online. This figure rose 26% from June 2006, as noted by digital survey company ComScore in its June 2007 United States Search Engine Rankings Report. ComScore also reports Google further increasing its search market share compared to the other mega search engines.[14] These statistics should serve as startling evidence for librarians to collaborate with the mega search engines, and especially with Google.

THE FOCUS ON GOOGLE

Since 2002, Google has been synonymous in the public mind with Internet Search. Google's recent inclusion as a verb in the "Oxford English Dictionary" confirms what all competitors, including reference librarians, feared: Google means Search to the majority of Internet users. The company has relied on word-of-mouth marketing and the ingenuity of its founders, Larry Page and Sergey Brin, to become a common household verb. To Google stands even more popular than the use of Xerox as a synonym for photocopying, and Kleenex as a synonym for tissues. Unlike Google, both older, long ago established companies actively condone the use of their trade marks as verbs, given that such use places the trademark in danger of being declared a generic term.

Google does not intend to rely on its past accomplishments or allow its lead against other Internet search engine competitors to wane. Ever striving to be all indexing, Google, in May 2007, announced its critical first steps toward a universal search model. This new search model promises users more integrated and comprehensive ways to search for and view information online. Marissa Mayer, Vice President of Search Products and User Experience at Google states, "The ultimate goal of universal search is to break down the silos of information that exist on the Web and provide the very best answer every time a user enters a query. While we still have a long way to go, today's announcements are a big step in that direction."[15]

Google's vision for universal search is ultimately to search across all its content sources, compare and rank all the information in real time, and deliver a single, integrated set of search results that offers users precisely what they are seeking. Google plans to subtly incorporate information from a variety of previously separate sources–including videos, images, news, maps, books, and Websites–into a single set of results. Over time users are promised recognition of additional types of content integrated into their search results as the company attempts to deliver a further comprehensive search experience.[16]

To further ease the rigors of Internet searching across countries and continents, Google, also in May 2007, unveiled a new cross-language search feature, Google Translate. Google Translate allows users across the world to find and view search results on foreign language Web pages in their own native language. By doing so, additional content on the Web is accessible to more users, regardless of what languages they speak. Reference librarians, working especially in multicultural environments, will find Google Translate beneficial. Google Translate is available in: English, Arabic, French, Italian, German, Spanish, Portuguese, Russian, Japanese, Korean, Chinese (Traditional), and Chinese (Simplified).[17]

To this end, Google is pouring the bulk of its resources into enhancing the breadth and quality of the search experience. Recent innovations involve wholly different methods of searching that may make today's Google seem primitive. As these projects evolve, the search mechanisms of the future will produce better answers to queries, much as the current Google is superior to the search engines that preceded it. "The ultimate search engine," says Page, "would understand exactly what you mean and give back exactly what you want."[18]

FALLING BY THE WAYSIDE

Yahoo!, the second largest search provider, at 26.8%, commands a market share more than double that of the next largest search engine, MSN. Outside of the top two search market share holders, MSN, Ask, and Time Warner Network (AOL) round out the top five search engines used in the United States. Yahoo's market share in terms of query volumes has declined over the last year as Google's brand draws away users. Yahoo! hopes to bring back users through social search, known as *Yahoo! Answers*.

Yahoo! also recently unveiled a new integrated brand campaign that demonstrates how Yahoo! can help people be better at whatever they're into. Whether it's being a better shopper, Frisbee player, or salesman, Yahoo! advertises to empower users to connect to their interests and passions and evolve that part of their lives through Yahoo!'s information, tools, and services. Much to the reference librarian's chagrin, Yahoo!'s multi-million dollar advertising campaign "Be a Better . . ." spotlights Yahoo!'s trademark irreverence about the academic and scholarly resources.

The "Be a Better . . ." campaign focuses on Yahoo! Answers and Yahoo! oneSearch, a new search service available on users' mobile phones. oneSearch showcases how people can enhance their lives by using Yahoo! to access the world's knowledge and make informed decisions from anywhere, anytime. The "Be a Better . . ." messaging will integrate into Yahoo! fans' lives through interactive ads and promotions, for example "Be a Better Globetrotter" (Yahoo! Travel) and "Be a Better Roadie" (Yahoo! Autos).[19]

Very little is appearing on the forefront of development at MSN, Ask. com, and the host of other search engines available on the Internet. MSN, in 2006, announced a number of new features and enhancements including an updated version of Windows Live and a Windows Live Toolbar. Windows Live Search includes Web search, as well as an image search, news search, RSS feeds, mail, local search, shopping, and MSN spaces, Microsoft's blogging service. New and updated search engine components were also available, including search history, clock, notepad, Live Favorites, stock quotes, weather, and MSN Infopane, to access MSN content. Unfortunately for MSN, similar features have been available in the past via numerous other sites, including Google.

FUTURE DECISIONS

Gazing into the crystal ball of the future, what resources and responsibilities will tomorrow's reference librarian command? How long will it be before Google and/or the mega search engines require fees for access? Many concerns have already presented themselves in the reference librarian community.

One concern arises as librarians include Google Scholar on library Web pages alongside subscription resources. Librarians are concerned they may be seen as promoting Google Scholar's use for subject searching of scholarly material as well as suggesting that it is equivalent to the

other indexes and databases listed.[20] Will the placement of Google Scholar search boxes on library Web pages affect the use of other resources?
Are librarians purposely or unintentionally putting themselves out of
business by doing so? Many librarians would agree in the affirmative to
both questions.

Among the many libraries with no intention of putting themselves
out of business are Baruch College Library in New York City, the University of Georgia Libraries, and Joyner Library at East Carolina University. At Baruch, electronic reference is at the forefront of student and
faculty research. Reliance on electronic search is evident not only in the
remarkable number of computer stations spread throughout the reference section, but also in the quantity of empty shelving units that formerly housed print sets and periodicals. The University of Georgia
Libraries report cancellation of all print indexes, in favor of Web-based
versions of the same materials. Both Baruch and Georgia universities
state they can meet most of their undergraduates' needs without a print
collection.[21] Joyner Library at East Carolina University has also switched
to electronic versions for most of its serial subscriptions. In addition,
Joyner Library has begun an ongoing series of Google drop-in sessions.
These 15 minute sessions, held twice per month, provide in-depth training on the many tricks and short cuts embedded in Google and Google
Scholar's search features. All three libraries are now actively marketing
their services to their communities, as they have learned to do from their
commercial counterparts.

CONCLUSION

As Paul Courant notes in his article "Scholarship and Academic Libraries (and their kin) in the World of Google," except for the most ar-
cane materials and users, that which is not available online will simply
not be read. Libraries must make sure true scholarly material is available online, or users will only see the inferior material. In addition, collaboration is the fundamental method of scholarship, and without it
libraries can do nothing of value. If libraries focus on the purposes and
mechanisms of scholarship, the new technologies should be our friends.

In order to remain relevant to their communities, libraries will need to
work together and decide which of the mega search engine offerings they
wish to promote, which they are prepared to pay for, and which to reject.
Libraries will be required to stand up for the principle of free and equal

access to content, and for the principle of high-quality index provision, because without those principles we are no longer running libraries.[22] It is important not to take sides, but to expend energy and resources on useful and valuable innovations within each library's grasp. Certainly a middle road exists between the old and the new reference services and it is highly conceivable for libraries to prosper in both worlds.

NOTES

1. Vartan Gregorian. American Library Association Annual Conference. Washington Convention Center, Washington, DC. June 23, 2007.

2. Benton Foundation. *Buildings, Books, and Bytes.* Washington, D.C.: Benton Foundation, 1996. <http://www.benton.org/publibrary/kellogg/buildings.html> (accessed June 3, 2007).

3. Ibid.

4. Maurice C. York. "Calling the Scholars Home: Google Scholar as a Tool for Rediscovering the Academic Library," *Internet Reference Services Quarterly*, 10:3/4 (2005): 118.

5. LibQUAL+ Survey, Greenville, NC: Joyner Library, East Carolina University, unpublished report, 2007, p. 38.

6. Nancy J. Becker. "Google in Perspective: understanding and enhancing student search skills." *The New Review of Academic Librarianship*, 9:1 (2003): 84.

7. Deborah Fallows, *Search Engine User*, Washington, D.C.: Pew Internet & American Life Project, 2005. <http://www.pewinternet.org/PPF/r/146/report_display. asp> (accessed April 27, 2007).

8. Ibid.

9. Benton Foundation. *Buildings, Books, and Bytes.* Washington, D.C.: Benton Foundation, 1996. <http://www.benton.org/publibrary/kellogg/buildings.html> (accessed June 4, 2007).

10. Richard Wayne. "T4: Top Texas Technology Trends," *Texas Library Journal*, Spring (2005): 13.

11. Janice S. Lewis. "Re: Google and Libraries." E-mail to the author. April 27, 2007.

12. Safa Rashtchy. *The User Revolution: The New Advertising Ecosytem and The Rise of the Internet as a Mass Medium.* East Palo Alto, CA: Piper Jaffray, (2007), p. 169.

13. John Battele. *The Search.* New York, NY: Portfolio, 2005.

14. Andrew Lipsman. *ComScore Releases may U.S. Search Engine Rankings.* Reston, VA: ComScore, Inc., 2007. <www.comscore.com/press/release.aps?press=1525> (accessed July 25, 2007).

15. "Google Begins Move to Universal Search." May 16, 2006. <http://www.google. com/intl/en/press/pressrel/univeralsearch_20070516.html> (accessed June 5, 2007).

16. "Google and Four US States Improve Public Access to Government Websites." *Google.* (April 30, 2007) <http://www.google.com/intl/en/press/pressrel/ govt_access.html.> (accessed June 5, 2007).

17. "Google Leaps Over Language Barriers." May 23, 2007. <http://www.google. com/intl/en/press/annc/translate_20070523.html.> (accessed June 5, 2007).

18. David A. Vise and Mark Malseed. *The Google Story.* New York, NY: Portfolio, 2005.

19. "Yahoo! Empowers Users To 'Be a Better . . .' " Through the Most Integrated Brand Campaign in Company History. April 30, 2007. <http://yhoo.client.shareholder. com/press/ReleaseDetail.cfm?ReleaseID=239962> (accessed June 4, 2007).

20. Laura Bowering Mullen and Karen A. Hartman. "Google Scholar and the Library Web Site: The Early Response by ARL Libraries." *College & Research Libraries*, 67:2 (March 2006):117.

21. Mirela Roncevic. "The e-Ref Invasion." *Library Journal*, 130:19 (2005):8.

22. John MacColl. "Google Challenges for Academic Libraries." *Ariadne, 46:64* (February2006) <http://www.ariadne.ac.uk/issue46/maccoll/> (accessed June 5, 2007).

REFERENCES

"Google and Four US States Improve Public Access to Government Websites." *Google,* (April 30, 2007) <http://www.google.com/intl/en/press/pressrel/govt_access.html> (accessed June 5, 2007).

"Google Begins Move to Universal Search." *Google*, (May 16, 2007). <http://www.google.com/intl/en/press/pressrel/univeralsearch_20070516.html> (accessed June 5, 2007).

"Google Leaps Over Language Barriers." *Google*, (May 23, 2007). <http://www.google.com/intl/en/press/annc/translate_20070523.html> (accessed June 5, 2007).

Battele, John. *The Search.* New York, NY: Portfolio, 2005.

Battele, John. "Web 2.0 Principles." (May 20, 2007). <http://www.federatedmedia.net/blog/> (accessed June 5, 2007).

Becker, Nancy J. "Google in Perspective: Understanding and Enhancing Student Search Skills." *New Review of Academic Librarianship*, 9 (2003): 84-100.

Benton Foundation. *Buildings, Books, and Bytes.* Washington, D.C.: Benton Foundation, 1996. <http://www.benton.org/publibrary/kellogg/buildings.html> (accessed June 4, 2007).

Brophy, Jan, and David Bawden. "Is Google Enough? Comparison of an Internet Search Engine with Academic Library Resources." *Aslib Proceedings*, 57:6 (2005): 498-512.

Courant, Paul N. "Scholarship and Academic Libraries (and their Kin) in the World of Google." *First Monday*, 11:8 (2006):1-14.

Fallows, Deborah. *Search Engine User.* Washington, D.C.: Pew Internet & American Life Project, 2005. <http://www.pewinternet.org/PPF/r/146/report_display.asp> (accessed April 27, 2007).

Gregorian, Vartan. American Library Association Annual Conference. Washington Convention Center, Washington, DC. June 23, 2007.

Lewis, Janice S. " Re: Google and Libraries." E-mail to the author. April 27, 2007.

LibQUAL+ Survey, Greenville, NC: Joyner Library, East Carolina University, unpublished report, 2007.

Lipsman, Andrew. *ComScore Releases may U.S. Search Engine Rankings.* Reston, VA: ComScore, Inc., 2007. <www.comscore.com/press/release.aps?press=1525> (accessed July 25, 2007).

MacColl, John. "Google Challenges for Academic Libraries." *Ariadne*, 46:64 (February 2006) <http://www.ariadne.ac.uk/issue46/maccoll/> (accessed June 5, 2007).

Mullen, Laura Bowering, and Karen A. Hartman. "Google Scholar and the Library Web Site: The Early Response by ARL Libraries." *College & Research Libraries,* 67 (2006): 106-122.

Rashtchy, Safa. *The User Revolution: The New Advertising Ecosytem and The Rise of the Internet as a Mass Medium.* East Palo Alto, CA: Piper Jaffray, 2007.

Roncevic, Mirela. "The e-Ref Invasion." *Library Journal*, 130:19 (2005): 8-10, 13.

Vise, David A., and Mark Marlseed. *The Google Story.* New York, NY: Delacorte Press, 2005.

Wayne, Richard. "T4: Top Texas Technology Trends for Libraries." *Texas Library Journal*, 81:1 (2005): 12-17.

"Yahoo! Empowers Users To 'Be a Better . . . '" Through the Most Integrated Brand Campaign in Company History. (April 30, 2007). <http://yhoo.client.shareholder.com/press/ReleaseDetail.cfm?ReleaseID=239962> (accessed June 4, 2007).

York, Maurice C. "Calling the Scholars Home: Google Scholar as a Tool for Rediscovering the Academic Library." *Internet Reference Services Quarterly*, 10:3/4 (2005): 117-123.

An Opportunity, Not a Crisis:
How Google Is Changing the Individual
and the Information Profession

Kay Cahill

INTRODUCTION

Do you remember the first time you Googled something? For me, the introduction came from a coworker at a library in Central London where I was working at the time. It was 1997, and we'd just had our staff computers connected to the net and were in the process of installing the first public Internet access terminals in the library. The Internet, and the myriad of information on it, still felt shiny and new.

Looking at the search interface that my coworker was so excitedly recommending, I remember feeling a little skeptical. It looked rather basic in comparison to the much more sophisticated search interfaces of

AltaVista and Lycos, my preferred search engines at the time. And yet within a search or two, I was converted. It was immediately apparent, even at that early stage, that Google was returning impressively relevant results with general, unplanned searches. In some cases, the loosely connected keywords were clearly providing better results lists than carefully planned Boolean searches on AltaVista.

This did not necessarily mean that Google was the best search engine for every kind of search, or that it was not worth putting the time into planning a structured search, but something that was–and remains–unique to Google is that Eureka moment: "the singular epiphany we all felt the first time we used Google" (Battelle 251, 2005).

BRAVE NEW WORLD

Ten years ago, many people were still finding their feet on the Web. They were still trying to work out how to map this unfamiliar environment, to navigate the strangely formed regions of cyberspace, to find a way of negotiating a system with no one in charge, no fixed rules, and no set structure–an organic, motile environment that was expanding exponentially by the day. A great description of the Internet from this era compares it to:

> the library you would expect to find in the type of gothic house you see in horror films: huge and rambling, with long corridors leading off into the middle of nowhere, small rooms packed with frequently used material in little order and yet other places shrouded in darkness from which one can hear rather nasty noises. The whole grand edifice is presided over by a half-insane librarian who is constantly coming up with new classification and cataloguing schemes. He then implements them on a few hundred titles before thinking of a new idea, and begins again with a different scheme on some new materials which have just been dumped on no order onto the floor. Meanwhile, minions of our insane librarian are busy working in different rooms, constantly arranging and rearranging their own collections, without reference to each other, and each convinced that they have the best collection and best scheme for its arrangement. (Bradley 2000)

For people who were not trained information professionals, figuring the net out was a challenge. They weren't necessarily sure what a search engine was or how to find one, nor did those people who did know about search engines know how to use them effectively. Google changed this beyond all recognition. All of a sudden, people didn't have to know how to Boolean search. A handful of keywords, and nine times out of ten they would be looking at a list of surprisingly relevant search results even if they knew nothing about how the net worked. I still find this when I'm teaching basic search skills to people who haven't used the Internet much–their eyes widen when they realize that with Google, it really is as easy as they thought it was going to be before they actually got online and were confronted with an unfamiliar interface and a strange environment. There's no question that Google's multi-algorithmic approach, which combines full text, metadata, and popularity measures, along with a bit of old-fashioned human evaluation, is the most successful approach any search engine has taken to producing relevant results.

This, however, is where reality intrudes. Google supplies such an abundance of results that it can make anyone think they're an information expert. With almost zero traditional advertising, simply through word-of-mouth, Google has become synonymous with Web searching and, for many people, with research itself: the "Google or bust" mentality. Many people now believe that finding the answer to a question is as simple as going to a single webpage, typing in a few keywords, and seeing what comes back. It's true that Google will almost always give you something, and generally quite useful somethings, but links are not the same as answers–and definitely not the same as authoritative answers.

Powerful though it is, Google is still an automated tool: it might be the most popular search engine around, but it still has many of the search engine's inherent frailties when it comes to sifting relevant material out of the masses of different taxonomies and indexing systems that exist on the Web. At the end of the day, Google supplies the results list: it is still down to the individual sat at the screen to assess the relevance and authority of the individual items on that list.

As companies and individuals grow increasingly adept at working within the PageRank scheme to ensure that their pages appear high on results lists, the danger is that users who has not been trained to recognize authority will rely on Google's results lists to tell them which site is preferred, and will end up choosing a site whose creator was the best at search engine optimization, rather than the best authority on the subject. We all know that these are the risks. The questions are: how serious are they, and what should we be doing about them?

MEETING THE NEED

The first of these two questions is the easiest to address. There is a whole new role for the information profession in the Google-driven world. As a gateway to information, we have the opportunity to teach users about authority, about optimizing searches, and about the areas where Google is not the be-all and end-all. There's also a second, even more interesting possibility: that our role is not just to act as a gateway between users and information, but as facilitators in finding new ways to process and share that information.

Stephen Berlin Johnson, author of *Everything Bad Is Good for You* and someone with his finger very much on the pulse of popular culture, argued eloquently in his keynote speech at the 2007 BCLA Conference that one of the biggest mistakes educators are making is not to test children on their information literacy skills: on their ability to navigate the Internet, carry out searches, and evaluate the results. Instead, they test them on their ability to solve algebraic equations–skills that will have little practical use for most people in their daily life as adults. Yet searching the net for information is something that the vast majority of adults in the developed world will do every day.

In a world where people are increasingly turning to the net for everything from preliminary medical diagnoses to business research, knowing how to separate the wheat from the chaff of search results is one of the most crucial skills a schoolchild can develop: and yet this kind of education remains at a fairly basic level in terms of both time and assessment. If children aren't tested in these skills, it's very hard to tell whether the way they are being taught right now is extensive or effective enough. In short, we're failing to ensure that children have the skills they will need in a world where enough information to overwhelm them is just the click of a button away.

This is an area where the library profession has invaluable experience and expertise to offer. It's what we do, what we've always done: making information more accessible. The fundamental difference is that in the past, we've been able to develop and fine-tune our own tools for doing the organization and categorization of information, and these tools have then driven the accessibility of the information. There is no question that we've done this well, but at the same time these tools have not always made sense to people outside of the profession. We've all been there and seen library patrons struggling with the intricacies of the Dewey Decimal System, or Library of Congress subject headings. Our primary instructional role in the traditional environment was to explain these librarian-developed tools and systems so that the end user could make enough sense of them to use them to access the information they needed. Our second role was to step in where the user's knowledge or comprehension ended, and do whatever else needed to be done to connect them with the information they were seeking.

Now, the environment has changed. The tools that are being used to organize, categorize, and search information are being created externally: by Google, by del.ici.ous, by the end users themselves. In many ways our role in this new environment is fundamentally the same: to instruct users in how to use these tools to access the information they need, and to step in and help when they hit barriers. The difference is that we're no longer in control of the tools that we're using to do this.

Is this a problem? Is it a bad thing, a threat to the integrity of our profession and our work? There are a lot of people who would argue that it is. Personally, I don't agree. I believe that this fundamental switch is creating opportunity for librarians on a scale absolutely unprecedented by anything in the profession's history. Essentially, using tools selected by the end user to teach them information skills is enabling us to engage people on a massive scale–and to do so far more effectively than we've ever been able to in the past. Google's success is in no small part due to the fact that it's incredibly simple, incredibly intuitive, and incredibly responsive. One small box, waiting for search terms: this is something that even the most novice computer user can understand. And even the most general searches, even the most obscure words, produce *results.*

Of course, there's an inherent danger–especially for new searchers–that these won't be very good results. There, of course, is the first opening for libraries and librarians: explaining how to find out whether or not the results are good, and if they're not, how to make them better. We can teach them how to use Google's advanced interface to narrow down those 275,000,000 hits. We can provide instruction on selecting search terms, on using Boolean operators, and on the different resources that may be a much faster and more effective route to the results they're looking for.

However, this is secondary. The biggest change of all in this searchable world is that even the newest Internet user thinks of himself/herself as a searcher, and knows that his/her searches will bring results. Thanks to the Internet, the general *awareness* of information has increased exponentially. Everyone knows it's out there, and everyone knows that the tools exist to find it.

In the old days, the danger would be that endless searches would produce little or even zero results. Users attempting to work with controlled vocabularies they didn't fully understand would eventually grow frustrated, and give up. The danger now is the opposite: that people will find themselves overwhelmed by results, unable to see the wood for the trees. As W. Bruce Cameron once said, "What use is a search engine that gives me 1,800,000 results? That's like saying 'Good news, we've found the product you're looking for. It's on earth.'" But something about this changing dynamic–the culture of more, rather than less–is changing the way users see themselves, and the way they see information. They see themselves as searchers, and they know that the information is out there. And they no longer see librarians as the guardians of information per se. They see librarians as the guardians of the expertise they need to use the tools they know are out there to access that information.

EVERYONE AN AUTHOR

The Internet has brought about profound changes in the way information is perceived, and in the way it is understood. The other paradigm shift is in the hole it has torn through conventional publishing. Now, anyone with access to a computer and basic typing skills can be an author. It takes just a minute or two to set up a personal blog using free online software like Blogger or Livejournal. The result is a wealth of random facts, opinions, and other unsourced information. This is one of the things that the Google naysayers argue so passionately against: that the sheer volume of information, and the tendency of the naïve searcher to assume that any list of search results produced by a search engine is in some way authoritative, mean people are liable to accept opinion as fact. An information professional would know that Dave's Blog, with its unverified facts and clearly biased opinions, was perhaps not as good a source as, say, a paper published on the Harvard University website. A naïve user would simply take whatever was at the top of the list at face value.

Another effect the abundance of information out there is having is that it's giving people a new understanding and sense of ownership of information. The fact is that if people know that they can publish their unsubstantiated opinion on a blog, they understand that other blogs out there may also be unsubstantiated opinion. And, to borrow another argument from Steven Johnson, all this opinion–even the misinformation–out there on the net isn't misleading us into devaluing facts. It's actually making us smarter.

When a hot political topic comes up, people read the news articles; but they also read the blogs. They read blogs not only written by the people commenting on these items from a distance, or through the variously colored lenses of politics or journalism, but blogs written by those who are intimately involved: civilians living the day-to-day reality of war, or soldiers serving on the front line. They absorb information, views, and opinions from across the world, ranging far outside the scope of the traditional social circle. For those who participate in discussion on hot topics or issues, suddenly having an opinion isn't enough: they also need to be able to defend that opinion. Internet discussion forums are traditionally not especially kind to people who quote opinion as fact, or fail to provide sources for their arguments.

Moreover, they draw on the experience and opinions of people from all over the world, from all kinds of backgrounds and cultures. All of this is forcing us to think things through as never before: to explore our opinions, the opinions of others, and the facts and sources that are giving us the information that drive those opinions. Our minds are open, the horizons are expanding, and the traditional geographical and physical barriers are crashing down around us. "A standard keyword search opens the widest of windows on the narrowest of topics. We have the power to inform ourselves like never before" (Morville 2006).

BORN FINDABLE

One particularly interesting thing is seeing the effect that all this information has had on the current generation, the ones who grew up never knowing a world without the Internet or a life without Google. For them, the world has always been searchable, and it has had a profound effect on the way they respond to and process information. In his excellent article, "Born With the Chip," Stephen Abram presents the nine key behavioural aspects of this generation. And the interesting thing is that they're not information illiterates, struggling to analyse and cope with the signal to noise ratio out there on the net. Instead, they have incorporated this glut of information–and the means of sifting through it and analyzing what they find–into their life experience. It's not the sudden, overwhelming change that it was for, for example, the baby boomers: it's simply the environment they have grown up with, and consequently it's one they know and understand.

Interestingly, one of the key features that Abram identifies is that this generation is principled. They show a much higher incidence of personal values such as veganism, political action, environmentalism, and volunteerism than previous generations. Abram discusses the impact this may have for libraries, but almost more important is the question: why? The answer lies in the points already discussed in this article. This generation has access to the widest range of opinions, facts, and discussion that has ever been open to anyone with a computer. They have grown up in a world where, when they are curious about a topic, they can literally press a button, type a few words, and access thoughts and opinions on that topic from all over the world. If they're unsure of how they feel about a political issue or current event, they can go to Google News and run a blog search and read about how it's affecting the people in its immediate vicinity, here and now.

The power of the keyword search–the power of Google–has quite literally brought innumerable realities to their door. This next generation of searchers is indifferent to form, able to handle multiple tasks at one time, quick to move on when they're not satisfied (partly because Google has encouraged them to embrace the immediate answer, but also because they take it for granted that there is more information out there to move on to), direct about what they think, and quick to adapt to new technologies and opportunities. They are, to quote Abram again, "a generation who have grown up in a Google World."

We do many of our users a grave disservice when we assume that they're so swamped by information that they can't figure out the fact from the fiction. In fact, we're dealing with the most tech-savvy, information aware generation that has ever lived. This answers the second part of our question: how serious are the risks posed by the information overload? The answer is that they're not as serious as we might think. The volume of information, and its accessibility through Google and its vast stable of spin-off tools, is not leading to a devaluing of information and the information profession. Instead, it's created a generation with a unique and unprecedented level of information awareness.

Nonetheless, there's always room for improvement. And that's where the information professional comes in. Where we're needed is to teach and hone the skills required to use these new tools effectively; to help users understand where their limitations lie, and to teach them the techniques that will enable them to work around these gaps; we're needed to teach the value of persistence, which is in danger of slipping into extinction. This is the real risk of a surfeit of Googling.

In "Ambient Findability," Peter Morville writes "What we find changes who we become" (2005). Never a truer word was written. What we find defines us, changes us, challenges us, forces us to re-evaluate who we are and what we do. When more information is more findable than ever before, when we look at a generation that has grown up in a Google world, it's not really a surprise that their attitude and approach to information is entirely different than the one we experienced when we were growing up. By Stephen Abram's definition, I missed out on being born with the chip by about six years. A part of me is sad about that; I think the current generation is extremely lucky to have grown up in the modern information environment. But a part of me is also glad, because it means I don't take any of this for granted. I remember how it was before, and my personal opinion is that this is better. Not being able to see the wood for the trees is far better than living on a scorched earth.

CONCLUSION

It's very easy to argue that Google is a bad thing. It's easy to argue that it's devaluing information, leading users to look for and accept the quick fix, and encouraging people to stop asking the kinds of questions that allow them to differentiate opinion and bias from proven facts. Nothing is ever black and white, and these are all things that are happening–but not among all Internet users. Not even among a majority of them. In fact, Google is leading many people to a greater understanding of the value of information–and more than that, of *access* to information–than ever before. Google is an opportunity, not a crisis.

Google is challenging us. It's forcing us to re-evaluate what we do, who we serve, and what being an information professional really means. It's forcing us to change. If you believe change is a negative, it becomes very easy to argue that Google is a bad thing, to bring out the often-repeated arguments that it's dumbing information down, that it's too easily manipulated by businesses and advertisers, that it simply encourages people to accept half-baked theories or random opinions as fact. But the world moves on, and we need to move with it. Change isn't necessarily bad; it's just different. And after all, if we don't change, how can we get better?

REFERENCES

Battelle, John. 2005. *The Search: How Google and Its Rivals Rewrote the Rules of Business and Changed our Culture.* New York: Penguin Books.

Bradley, Phil. 2000. *The Advanced Internet Searcher's Handbook, 2nd Edition.* London: Library Association.

Johnson, Steven Berlin. 2007. *Keynote Address.* Burnaby: 2007 British Columbia Library Conference.

Morville, Peter. 2005. *Ambient Findability.* Sebastopol: O'Reilly Media.

Studying Journal Coverage
in Google Scholar

Philipp Mayr
Anne-Kathrin Walter

INTRODUCTION

As is now customary for new Google offerings, the launch of Google Scholar <http://scholar.google.com/> generated a great deal of media attention shortly after its debut in November 2004. Its close relation to the highly discussed topics of open access and invisible Web (Lewandowski and Mayr, 2006) ensured that many lines were devoted to this service in both the general media (Markoff, 2004; Terdiman, 2004) and among scientific publishers and scientific societies (Banks, 2004; Butler, 2004; Payne, 2004; Sullivan, 2004; Jacsó, 2004; Giles, 2005). While the initial euphoria over this new service from Google has since quieted down, the service is currently being used by academic searchers to retrieve results that are available free of charge.

Google Scholar stands out not just for the technology employed but for the efforts made to restrict searches to scientific papers. As stated on the Google Scholar Webpage:

> Google Scholar enables you to search specifically for scholarly literature, including peer-reviewed papers, theses, books, preprints, abstracts and technical reports from all broad areas of research. Use Google Scholar to find articles from a wide variety of academic publishers, professional societies, preprint repositories and universities, as well as scholarly articles available across the web. (Google 2005, see <http://scholar.google.com/scholar/about.html>)

Above all, it appears that Google is attempting to automatically index the totality of the realm of scientifically relevant documents with this new search service Google Scholar. As Google does not make any information available with regard to coverage or how current the content it offers is, this study has been undertaken with the goal of empirically exploring the depth of search in the scientific Web. We have measured the coverage of the service by testing different journal lists. The types of results and which Web servers are represented in the result are also analyzed.

The paper first describes the background, functions and unique features of Google Scholar. A brief literature review will bring together the current research results. Results of the second Google Scholar study from August 2006 will be presented in the second part. An initial analysis of journals in Google Scholar was conducted in the period April/May 2005 (Mayr and Walter, 2006). The results of this study were compared with certain parts of the current analysis in August 2006. This is followed by a summary of our observations on this new service.

GOOGLE SCHOLAR

The pilot project CrossRef Search <http://www.crossref.org/cross refsearch.html> can be seen as a test and predecessor of Google Scholar.

For CrossRef Search Google indexed full-text databases of a large number of academic publishers such as Blackwell, Nature Publishing Group, Springer, etc., and academic/professional societies such as the Association for Computing Machinery, the Institute of Electrical and Electronics Engineers, the Institute of Physics, etc., displaying the results via a typical Google interface. The CrossRef Search interface continues to be provided by various CrossRef partners (e.g., at Nature Publishing Group).

Similar in approach, but broader and less specific in scope than Google Scholar, the scientific search engine Scirus <http://www.scirus. com> searches, according to information it provides, approximately 300 million science-specific Web pages. In addition to costly scientific documents from Elsevier (ScienceDirect server, see <http://www.science direct.com/>), freely accessible documents, many from public Web servers at academic institutions are also provided. Among these are, for example, documents placed by students that do not fulfill scientific criteria, such as peer review, which often lead to their exclusion in searches. In our experience there is more than a negligible fraction of records from non-academic Web spaces in the Scirus index. Scirus' coverage of purely scientific sources in addition to Elsevier's ScienceDirect full-text collection is comparably low (see e.g., the selection of hosts in the Scirus advanced search interface, <http://scirus.com/srsapp/advanced/>). What Scirus declares as the "rest of the scientific web" is too general, non-specifically filtered and makes up the majority of hits in any query.

As seen in the pilot project CrossRef Search, the chosen Google Scholar approach is to work in cooperation with academic publishers. What is significant about the Google Scholar approach?

First and foremost, what stands out is that Google Scholar, as previously mentioned, delivers results restricted to exclusively scientific documents and this constraint has yet to be consistently implemented by any other search engine provider. Google Scholar is a freely available service with a familiar interface similar to Google Web Search. Much of the content indexed by Google Scholar is stored on publishers' servers where full-text documents can be downloaded for a fee, but at least the abstracts of the documents found will be displayed at no cost. Secondarily the Google approach does provide documents from the open access and self-archiving areas (compare Swan and Brown, 2005).

In addition to the full-text access users might also be interested in the analysis implemented by Google and the document ranking based on this analysis. The relevance ranking is based on various criteria (see citation below). According to this the citation value of a document is only one factor contributing to its ranking. Google builds a citation index out of the full-text index as an add-on to its service. On top of the statistical best match ranking of full texts, this add-on implementation can be valuable for re-ranking documents or for analysis and evaluation purposes of certain document sets. Automatic reference extraction and analysis, also known as Autonomous Citation Indexing (ACI), can be particularly helpful for the user in information retrieval and delivery. This process ensures that often cited scientific works will be ranked more highly in the results list, thereby making them more visible to the user. Additionally the user can track all citing works extracted by ACI which need not necessarily be included in the full-text index or contain the original user search term. The automatic ACI process necessitates that references in the documents analyzed be available, which is, per se, for granted if full texts with references are analyzed. This procedure also enables Google Scholar to present additional references not found on the indexed web servers.

Figure 1 is a graphic representation of the Google Scholar approach including the value added service ACI. See three different citing styles for the same reference in Lawrence, Giles and Bollacker (1999) that are intended to illustrate the difficulties in dealing with automatic normalization of references. The original system CiteSeer <http://citeseer.ist. psu.edu/> as well as Google Scholar have up to now implemented only heuristics for the application of ACI that also produce some errors in the citation values (see also Jacsó, 2005c, 2006a, 2006b).

Google Scholar is also noteworthy for the fact that it is conceived of as an interdisciplinary search engine. In contrast to specialty search engines like the CiteSeer system which indexes freely available computer science literature or RePEc for economic papers, the Google Scholar approach can be conceived of as a comprehensive science search engine.

The following is a short description of the most important features of Google Scholar:

- *Advanced search:* The advanced search offers, in addition to searching the title of the article, the opportunity to search for an author name, journal title, and year of publication of an article or book (see Jacsó, 2005a, 2005b for details on the limitations). These attributes represent only a minimal set of search criteria compared to specifically scientific search interfaces and the reliable extraction of this data from un- or only partially structured documents poses a

FIGURE 1. Google Scholar Approach

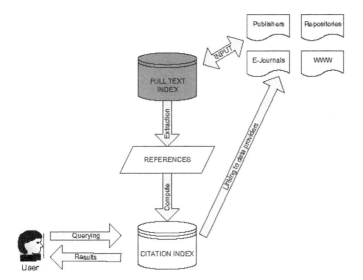

serious problem for an automatic system. The advanced search has recently begun to offer access by subject to different disciplines.

- *Full-text access:* In contrast to the classical abstracting and indexing databases, which search in bibliographic metadata, including abstract and keywords, Google Scholar searches based on a full-text index. This means that the user can–with minor limitations (Price, 2004) and all the advantages and disadvantages of this kind of search–directly search and access the full text of documents.
- *Relevance ranking:* Relevance statement by Google (2004): "Just as with Google Web Search, Google Scholar orders your search results by how relevant they are to your query, so the most useful references should appear at the top of the page. This relevance ranking takes into account the full text of each article as well as the article's author, the publication in which the article appeared and how often it has been cited in scholarly literature. Google Scholar also automatically analyzes and extracts citations and presents them as separate results, even if the documents they refer to are not online. This means your search results may include citations of older works

and seminal articles that appear only in books or other offline publications." (Google 2004, see <http://web.archive.org/web/2004 1130084532/scholar.google.com/scholar/about.html>). The relevance statement offered by Google in 2004 has since been shortened to the following: "Google Scholar aims to sort articles the way researchers do, weighing the full text of each article, the author, the publication in which the article appears, and how often the piece has been cited in other scholarly literature. The most relevant results will always appear on the first page." (Google 2007, see <http:// scholar.google.de/intl/en/scholar/about.html>).

- *Web search:* The link to the Google main index is useful especially when the documents are not directly available from the Google Scholar result list and the query is expanded to the whole (Google) web.
- *Institutional access:* The pilot project Institutional Access mainly offers additional value for institutional users such as students or scientific staff as Google uses open linking/link resolver such as SFX to link directly to local library holdings.
- *Additional features:* Google Scholar offers additional features like *Library Search* which links the query to OCLC WorldCat (http:// www.oclc.org/worldcat/) thereby providing hits from local libraries. Alternative places of a document on the web will also be presented.

HOW DEEP DOES GOOGLE SCHOLAR DIG?

Much criticism has already been leveled at the lack of information about the actual size and coverage of Google Scholar (Jacsó, 2004, 2005a, 2005b; Mayr and Walter, 2006). Remaining questions as to how often the search engine index is truly updated can not be answered from publicly accessible research sources.

We would like to preface our journal title study of Google Scholar by giving a brief literature review of related studies published since the launch of Scholar. In our view there are at least two types of literature attempting to challenge Google Scholar in an academic way. There are papers analyzing the functionality, coverage and up-to-dateness of the Scholar service and there are studies using Scholar as an instrument and alternative tool for citation analysis.

Peter Jacsó began early on with his reviews of Scholar. In his critical commentaries (2004, 2005a, 2005b, 2005c) he pointed out that important features of academic search services like accurate searching of journal names (including name abbreviations), Boolean logic or publication years can be quite annoying and contain lots of mistakes in Scholar. The same problems arise in trying to count citations or hits (2006a, 2006b).

> Those who need a comprehensive set of papers that includes the most respected (and hence most-cited) articles, books and conference papers are advised to treat the hits–and citedness scores–in Google Scholar with much reservation. (Jacsó, 2005b)

His observations led him to conclude that Scholar could be a useful service if its implementation would be more careful and elaborated, but in its current beta status Scholar is not sufficient for scholarly research.

Beside arguments of functionality and accuracy, in our eyes there are the increasingly critical points of size, coverage, completeness, and up-to-dateness to be noted when using Scholar as a search tool. Google fails here, because it gives too little information about its sources. Some other researchers and professional searchers analyzing size, coverage, etc. have also registered their concerns about this policy (Noruzi, 2005; Bauer and Bakkalbasi, 2005; Mayr and Walter, 2006).

Another problem arises from lack of documentation.

> However, it is important for all researchers to note that until Google Scholar gives a full account of what material it is indexing and how often that index is updated, it cannot be considered a true scholarly resource in the sense that Web of Science and Scopus are. An understanding of the material being covered is central to the validity of any search of scholarly material. (Bauer and Bakkalbasi, 2005)

It can be said that Google Scholar covers only a part of the indexed document collections. The extent of this difference is often great (see Jacsó, 2005c), but it is difficult to explain it in a statistically correct way (compare Mayr and Tosques, 2005 for analyses with the Google APIs Web service). We assume that Google Scholar was started by only indexing a part of holdings. Preliminary and non-representative results of these experimental studies–including author, journal or topical searches–underscore the beta status of the Google Scholar service leading to the conclusion that presently the index is irregularly updated and completeness and up-to-dateness vary greatly between different collections.

Google Scholar is also drawing attention from literature coming from the fields of bibliometrics and informetrics. Researchers from this field compare the new Google Scholar service with the established citation indices Web of Science (WoS) and Scopus (Bauer and Bakkalbasi, 2005; Belew, 2005; Noruzi, 2005; Kousha and Thelwall, forthcoming) or other citation databases (e.g., CiteSeer, see Bar-Ilan, 2006). Most of these studies are based on small samples and applying different methodologies. Bauer and Bakkalbasi stated that "Google Scholar provided statistically significant higher citation counts than either Web of Science or Scopus," but this result is based on the analysis of only one journal and two different journal volumes. They also say that older material from the analyzed journal is covered better by WoS. Belew (2005) applauds the "first independent confirmation of impact data" but also identifies significant variations in the counts between the ISI/WoS and the Google citation database.

Belew and Bauer and Bakkalbasi also mentioned that Google Scholar could possibly cover the Open Access/self-archiving Web publishing fraction better than the traditional citation activity WoS. Noruzi (2005) compared citation counts for highly cited papers in the webometrics field. He found a certain overlap between Scholar and WoS and a good ratio of additional papers for Google Scholar. Kousha and Thelwall compared traditional and Web-based citation patterns of Open Access articles in multiple disciplines. They found "significant correlations and overlaps between ISI/WoS citations and both Google Scholar and Google Web/URL citations" in all disciplines studied. Correlation between ISI/WoS citations and Google Scholar citations is stronger than ISI/WoS correlated with Google Web citations. Kousha and Thelwall concluded from their interesting study that it could be said that Google Scholar had a "widely applicable value in citation counting," but that Scholar's limitations must also be noted.

Our study was carried out as an alternative attempt to create a more accurate picture of Google Scholar's current situation. Compared with the former studies, it utilizes a brute force approach to give a more macroscopic view on the content indexed by Scholar. Our study uses brute force in the sense that we gathered a lot of data from Google, and analyzed the data in a macroscopic fashion. The following study addresses the question: How deep does Google Scholar dig? The study should make it possible to answer these research questions:

- How complete is Google Scholar's coverage of different scientific journals on a general level? By querying multiple journal lists the study tests whether Google Scholar has indexed the journals and can display the articles. The journal lists come from widely varying subject areas: international peer-reviewed journals from the Web of Science <http://scientific.thomson.com/products/wos/> (particularly Science, Technology & Medicine), Open Access and social sciences, and enable conclusions to be drawn about the thematic focus of the current Google Scholar offering. Is Scholar touching the academic invisible Web (compare Lewandowski and Mayr, 2006)?

• Which document types does Google Scholar deliver? Are theses results sufficient for professional searchers and academic researching? The analyzed data gives indications about the composition and utility of the results delivered by Scholar: full text, link, and citation.

• From which providers does Google Scholar take the bulk of the documents retrieved? The study should show who the most prominent providers of data for this new service are, and which sources for scientific information are actually underrepresented in the index. The distribution and frequency of specific Web servers and content providers is significant as it is an indicator of whether Google Scholar delivers more pay-per document or freely accessible documents.

METHODOLOGY

In August of 2006 five different journal lists were queried and the results returned were analyzed. In most scientific disciplines journals are the most important forum for scientific discussion; they can be readily processed and a relatively small number of journals yields a representative and evaluable amount of results.

Since not all existing journals could be queried, a selection was made from these readily available journal lists.

• Journal lists from Thomson Scientific (ISI, see <http://scientific.thomson.com/mjl/>).

   o Arts & Humanities Citation Index (AH = 1,149 Titles) contains journals from the Humanities
   o Social Sciences Citation Index (SSCI = 1,917 Titles) contains international social science journals
   o Science Citation Index (SCI = 3,780 Titles) contains journals from Science/Technology and Medicine

- Open Access journals from the Directory of Open Access Journals (DOAJ, see <http://www.doaj.org/>). At the time of the study this list encompassed a total of 2,346 international Open Access Journals from all scientific fields.
- Journals from the SOLIS database (IZ, Sozialwissenschaftliches Literaturinformationssystem, see <http://www.gesis.org/Information/Zeitschriften/index.htm>). This list encompasses a total of 317 mainly German language journals from various sociological disciplines and related areas.

The five journal lists cover very different areas and cannot be directly compared in terms of content, range, and size. More insight should be gained regarding which scientific disciplines, in what form, and to what depth can be reached by Google Scholar. It should be noted that the five journal lists analyzed reflect only a small number of regularly appearing journals. The Electronic Journals Library <http://www.bibliothek.uni-regensburg.de/ezeit/> in Regensburg, Germany for example, covers more than 22,800 periodical titles, of which more than 2,650 are purely online journals. Harnad et al. (2004) arrive at a figure of approximately 24,000 peer-reviewed journals. Other estimates set the figure at about 100,000 periodically appearing publications (Ewert and Umstätter, 1997).

The study is divided into the following steps:

- *Step 1:* Querying the journal titles: Titles from all journal lists were queried to determine the coverage of Google Scholar. The aforementioned lists were queried in August, 2006. Advanced search offers the field "Return articles published in . . ."
- *Step 2:* Downloading of Google Scholar result pages: A maximum of 100 records were downloaded for every journal title to be processed.
- *Step 3:* Data extraction from the results list: the data studied are based on the individual records of the results pages. To clearly illustrate the approach, the typical structure of a Google Scholar hit is described in the following paragraph below.
- *Step 4:* Analysis and aggregation of the extracted data. The extracted data was aggregated using simple counts. We first counted each journal whose title could either be clearly identified or not. The results which could be matched were ordered according to the four different types of documents and counted. For each result matched to a journal, all domains were extracted and the frequency of the individual Web servers per journal list was computed (see Table 3).

Composition of Google Scholar Records

A typical Google Scholar record shows the following components:

- Title and document type of the record
- Domain of the Web server
- Citation count of the document
- Journal title

Title and Document Type of the Record

In addition to the relevance of a reference users are also interested in the availability of documents. The best case scenario is when users are directly linked to the full text; less favorable is when only a citation is displayed with the opportunity to query further via Google Web Search. The first line determines the type of the record. Certain types of documents are marked by brackets in front of the actual title to indicate their type.

- *Direct link to full text in Postscript- or PDF-Format:* Indicates a full-text record in Postscript or PDF-Format; "PS" or "PDF," respectively, appearing as prefix in brackets. This is not always the case for PDF-files so the suffix of the link must also be taken into consideration.
- *"Normal" reference:* Most of the records are links, leading first to a bibliographic reference which, according to Google Scholar, should contain at least one abstract.
- *Citations:* Many journal articles are offered by Google Scholar only as a citation. These results are denoted by the attached prefix "CITATION" and are not backed up by a link.
- *Books:* Google Scholar also delivers books as results, denoted by "BOOK." As this study is only concerned with references found in journals these will not be considered.

Domains

If the record is a link, the main Web server is denoted. If there are multiple sources, these can be reached by clicking the link "group of xy." These links were not included in the analysis; we only analyzed the main link for each linked record.

Citation Count

Document ranking by Google Scholar is partially based on article citation counts. These are displayed in the data but were not evaluated for this study.

Journal Title

Google Scholar supports phrase search in limited fashion so journals will be searched and displayed which do not necessarily contain the search term as a phrase. For this reason every record was individually checked and only counted as a hit when the exact title was found.

RESULTS

Identification of Journals

First, we checked how many journal titles from the lists could be identified by Google Scholar. Journals were only classed as "Titles found" (see Table 1) when they were clearly identifiable on the returned data. All titles not clearly identifiable were labeled as "Titles not found."

Table 1 shows that the majority of requested journal titles from the five lists (AH, DOAJ, IZ, SCI, SSCI) can be identified in the data delivered from Google Scholar (see Titles found column; average is approximately 78.5%), and that articles in the journals could actually be found. The exact number of the individual articles of a journal could not be determined because our analysis included only 100 hits for each journal. From the 317 journals on the IZ journal list (SOLIS) 222 titles (about 70% of the list) can be clearly identified (see "Titles found"). The remaining 30% of the list can not be clearly identified, or produce no hits. There was, interestingly, a relatively high number of journal titles found for all lists. Yet, surprisingly, only 67.9% of the freely accessible, open access journals can be definitively identified (see DOAJ list). The values of the DOAJ lists have fallen by about 10% when compared with our previous study in April/May 2005 (Mayr and Walter, 2006). The journals from Thomson Scientific (AH, SCI, SSCI) which are mainly English language journals, have the best coverage/identification percentage rate, at more than 80%.

Distribution of Document Types

We then analyzed Google Scholar data in terms of the document type to which it belongs. In total 621,000 Google Scholar records were ana-

TABLE 1. Identification of Journal Titles in Google Scholar Data

List	Titles	Titles Found (%)
AH	1,149	925 (80.50)
DOAJ	2,346	1,593 (67.90)
IZ	317	222 (70.03)
SCI	3,780	3,244 (85.82)
SSCI	1,917	1,689 (88.11)

lyzed. The Google Scholar hits can be categorized into four different types (Link, Citation, PDF-Link and other formats such as PS, DOC, RTF). The distribution of document types is closely related to the results described above. The high ratio of journals found is reflected in the high percentage of document type *Citation* (28%). This type, which Google terms "offline-record," cannot be described as a classical reference because it comprised extracted references and offers only minimal bibliographic information. The document type *Link*, a literature reference with an abstract, appears in the analyzed data with the largest ratio at approximately 53%. The references with direct access to full text in the pdf format (full text) are clearly less often represented, reaching only 19%. The other formats have negligible ratios. Our previous study (April/May 2005) showed similar values for both of the main document types (*Link* and *Citation*) of about 44% (compare Mayr and Walter, 2006). Based on these figures we conclude that the content coverage of the service has been expanded in 2006.

The values of the document types from the results analysis are detailed separately for each journal list in Table 2.

What stands out here is that the SOLIS database journals (see IZ, German language social science journals) generate, for the most part, only citations as results (see 83.11% under document types *Citation*). The reason is that Google Scholar cannot (directly) link the mostly German language articles and so offers only the extracted references from indexed documents. The ratio of citations from the international journal lists (DOAJ, AH, SCI, SSCI) is clearly lower but also, to some extent, relatively high (see lists AH with 50.7% citations). Approximately 30% of open access articles (DOAJ) could not be listed as full text or links. The international STM journals from Thomson Scientific (SCI) display the highest percentage of link references (approximately 61%). A no-

TABLE 2. Distribution of Document Types Among the Lists Queried

Lists	Link (%)	Citations (%)	Full-text (%)
AH	41.78	50.73	7.49
DOAJ	48.29	29.61	22.11
IZ	10.42	83.11	6.48
SCI	61.35	16.72	21.94
SSCI	49.38	32.84	17.78

ticeable increase in the document type link can be seen for all lists when compared with our previous study (April/May 2005).

Distribution of Web Servers

If a result links to a hyperlinked reference (document type link or full text) the distribution of this Web server can be evaluated per journal list and a frequency distribution computed.

Table 3 shows the 25 servers most frequently offering journal articles of the SCI list. The description column categorizes the type of server. *Publisher* indicates a commercial server offered by an academic publisher where there is a fee for full-text downloads; *Scientific portal* stands for servers offering free references and full texts, although they do not always link directly to the full text in every case. For some there may be more than a single appropriate description; for example, <poral. acm.org> is a publisher and scientific portal. *Open Access* describes open access servers which deliver full text free of charge.

The frequency of publishers at the top of the list which can be connected to Google Scholar's cooperation with publishers and CrossRef partners is noteworthy.

Table 4 displays the ten most frequent Web servers for all queried lists (AH, DOAJ, IZ, SCI, SSCI).

CONCLUSIONS

We are well aware that statements and conclusions included here possibly will need to be revised following the next Google Scholar update. All results and conclusions in this study are current and based

TABLE 3. Distribution of the 25 Most Frequent Web Servers (SCI List)

Web Server	Host Name	Description	Frequency
www.springerlink.com	Springer-Verlag	Publisher	33,148
cat.inist.fr	Catalog of the Institut de l'Information Scientifique et Technique	Scientific portal	30,495
www.ingentaconnect.com	Ingenta	Publisher	29,273
doi.wiley.com	Wiley	Publisher	12,202
www.blackwell-synergy.com	Blackwell	Publisher	11,344
www.csa.com	CSA	Publisher	11,075
www.ncbi.nlm.nih.gov	National Center for Biotechnology Information	Scientific portal	9,404
taylorandfrancis.metapress.com	Taylor & Francis Group	Publisher	8,180
linkinghub.elsevier.com	Elsevier	Publisher	7,368
adsabs.harvard.edu	Smithsonian/NASA Astrophysics Data System	Scientific portal	4,771
Links.jstor.org	JSTOR	Scientific portal	4,279
content.karger.com	Karger Publishers	Publisher	3,500
portal.acm.org	Portal of the Association for Computing Machinery	Scientific portal	3,207
ieeexplore.ieee.org	Portal IEEE	Scientific portal	2,353
www.nature.com	Nature Publishing Group	Publisher	2,190
link.aip.org	American Institute of Physics	Scientific portal	2,144
Pubs.acs.org	American Chemical Society	Scientific portal	2,083
www.iop.org	Institute of Physics	Scientific portal	1,280
www.liebertonline.com	Mary Ann Liebert	Publisher	1,234
www.journals.cambridge.org	Cambridge University Press	Publisher	1,161
www.journals.uchicago.edu	University of Chicago Press	Publisher	851
www.thieme-connect.com	Georg Thieme Verlag	Publisher	689
www.publish.csiro.au	CSIRO	Publisher	672
www.pubmedcentral.nih.gov	National Institute of Health	Open Access	667
pubs.rsc.org	Royal Society of Chemistry	Scientific portal	610

on sample tests (100 hits per query) and are valid as of January 2007. Like the widely used, familiar search service Google Web Search, Google Scholar offers fast searching with a simple, user-friendly interface. The pros of this are that the search is free of charge and is done across interdisciplinary full-text collections. The Google Scholar approach of-

TABLE 4. Top 10 Web Servers per Journal List

	AH	DOAJ	IZ	SCI	SSCI
1	links.jstor.org	www.scielo.br	cat.inist.fr	www.springerlink.com	links.jstor.org
2	cat.inist.fr	cat.inist.fr	www.springerlink.com	cat.inist.fr	www.ingentaconnect.com
3	muse.jhu.edu	www.biomedcentral.com	links.jstor.org	www.ingentaconnect.com	www.springerlink.com
4	www.questia.com	www.pubmedcentral.nih.gov 00	cesifo.oxfordjournals.org	doi.wiley.com	cat.inist.fr
5	www.springerlink.com	www.csa.com	www.psyjournals.com	www.blackwell-synergy.com	www.eric.ed.gov
6	www.ingentaconnect.com	redalyc.uaemex.mx	www.psycontent.com	www.csa.com	taylorandfrancis.metapress.com
7	www.blackwell-synergy.com	www.bioline.org.br	www.ingentaconnect.com	www.ncbi.nlm.nih.gov	www.blackwell-synergy.com
8	taylorandfrancis.metapress.com	www.hindawi.com	www.demographic-research.org	taylorandfrancis.metapress.com	www.questia.com
9	www.eric.ed.gov	www.emis.ams.org	www.cesifo-group.de	linkinghub.elsevier.com	doi.wiley.com
10	www.journals.cambridge.org	www.scielo.cl	hsr-trans.zhsf.uni-koeln.de	adsabs.harvard.edu	ideas.repec.org

fers some potential for literature retrieval; for example, automatic citation analysis and the ranking built up from this, and oftentimes direct downloading of full text which is sometimes also described as a subversive feature (listing of self-archived pre- and postprints). Accurate citation analysis and webometric studies based on Google Scholar data (see e.g., Belew, 2005; Noruzi, 2005; Bar-Ilan, 2006; Kousha and Thelwall, forthcoming; see also Webometrics Ranking of World Universities, <http://www.webometrics.info/methodology.html>) can be recommended only with some limitation due to a lot of inconsistencies and vagueness (compare Jacsó, 2006a, 2006b) in the data. Citation counts aggregated by Google Scholar may work in some fields which are covered and indexed quite well, but in other fields which are perhaps more represented by the freely accessible Web these counts can be very inflated. This can mislead researchers in citation analyses based solely on Google Scholar.

The study shows that the majority of the journals on the five lists queried can be retrieved in Google Scholar. Upon closer examination the results are relativized by the high percentage of extracted references (see Table 2, values of the document type citation). The international journals from the Thomson Scientific List (particularly from the area of STM) are fairly well covered. Analysis of the Web servers shows that the majority of the analyzed hits come from publishers. It seems that preference has been given to the collections of the CrossRef partners as well as additional commercial publishers partly indexed by Google Scholar (see Tables 3 and 4). As tested with the social science list (IZ) the ratio of German language journals is probably very low.

Our results show that the expanding sector of open access journals (DOAJ list) is underrepresented among the servers. Something that remains unclear is why journal articles that are freely available on Web servers are not readily listed by Google Scholar even though they are searchable via the classic Google Web Search. Although Google Scholar claims to provide "scholarly articles across the web," the ratio of articles from open access journals or the full text (eprints, preprints) is comparably low.

Concerning the question of up-to-dateness, our tests show that Google Scholar is not able to present the most current data. It appears that the index is not updated regularly. The coverage and up-to-dateness of individual, specific Web servers varies greatly. Our journal list queries empirically confirm Peter Jacsó's experience (Jacsó, 2005c) concerning the coverage of Google Scholar. This needs to be qualified by stating that the service is still in beta status. However this does not entirely explain deficits such as duplicates in results data, faulty results sets, and some non-scientific sources.

In comparison with many abstracting and indexing databases, Google Scholar does not offer the transparency and completeness to be expected from a scientific information resource. Google Scholar can be helpful as a supplement to retrieval in abstracting and indexing databases mainly because of its coverage of freely accessible materials.

REFERENCES

Banks, M. A. (2005), "The excitement of Google Scholar, the worry of Google Print," *Biomed Digit Libr.,* Vol. 2 No. 2, accessed July 28, 2007 <http://www.bio-diglib.com/content/2/1/2>.

Bar-Ilan, J. (2006), "An ego-centric citation analysis of the works of Michael O. Rabin based on multiple citation indexes," *Information Processing & Management,* Vol. 42 No. 6, pp.1553-1566.

Bauer, K. and Bakkalbasi, N. (2005), "An examination of citation counts in a new scholarly communication environment," *D-Lib Magazine*, Vol. 11 No. 9, accessed July 28, 2007 <http://www.dlib.org/dlib/september05/bauer/09bauer.html>.

Belew, R. K. (2005), "Scientific impact quantity and quality: Analysis of two sources of bibliographic data," accessed July 28, 2007 <http://arxiv.org/abs/cs.IR/0504036>.

Butler, D. (2004), "Science searches shift up a gear as Google starts Scholar engine," *Nature,* Vol. 432, p 423.

Ewert, G. and Umstätter, W. (1997), *Lehrbuch der Bibliotheksverwaltung*, Stuttgart: Hiersemann.

Giles, J. (2005), "Science in the web age: Start your engines," *Nature,* Vol. 438 No. 7068, pp. 554-555.

Harnad, S., Brody, T., Vallières, F., Carr, L., Hitchcock. S., Gingras, Y., Oppenheim, C., Stamerjohanns, H. and Hilf, E. (2004), "The green and the gold roads to Open Access," *Nature*, accessed July 28, 2007 <http://www.nature.com/nature/focus/accessdebate/21.html>.

Jacsó, P. (2004), "Google Scholar Beta," Thomson Gale, accessed July 28, 2007 <http://www.galegroup.com/servlet/HTMLFileServlet?imprint=9999&region=7&fileName=/reference/archive/200412/googlescholar.html>.

Jacsó, P. (2005a), "As we may search - Comparison of major features of the Web of Science, Scopus, and Google Scholar citation-based and citation-enhanced databases," *Current Science,* Vol. 89 No. 9, pp.1537-1547.

Jacsó, P. (2005b), "Google Scholar Beta (Redux)," Thomson Gale, accessed July 28, 2007 <http://www.gale.com/servlet/HTMLFileServlet?imprint=9999&region=7&fileName=/reference/archive/200506/google.html>.

Jacsó, P. (2005c), "Google Scholar: the pros and the cons," *Online Information Review,* Vol. 29 No. 2, pp. 208-214.

Jacsó, P. (2006a), "Deflated, Inflated and Phantom Citation Counts," *Online Information Review,* Vol. 30 No. 3, pp. 297-309.

Jacsó, P. (2006b), "Dubious Hit Counts and Cuckoo's Eggs," *Online Information Review,* Vol. 30 No. 2, pp.188-193.

Kousha, K. and Thelwall. M. (2007), "Google Scholar citations and Google Web/URL citations: A multi-discipline exploratory analysis," *Journal of the American Society for Information Science and Technology,* Vol. 58 No. 7, pp. 1055-1065.

Lawrence, S., Giles, C. L. and Bollacker, K. (1999), "Digital Libraries and Autonomous Citation Indexing," *IEEE Computer,* Vol. 32 No. 6, pp. 67-71, accessed July 28, 2007<http://citeseer.ist.psu.edu/aci-computer/aci-computer99.html>.

Lewandowski, D. and Mayr, P. (2006), "Exploring the academic invisible web," *Library Hi Tech,* Vol. 24 No. 4, pp. 529-539, accessed July 28, 2007 <http://conference.ub.uni-bielefeld.de/2006/proceedings/lewandowski_mayr_final_web.pdf>.

Markoff, J. (2004), "Google Plans New Service For Scientists And Scholars," *The New York Times,* Section Technology, published November 18, 2004, C6.

Mayr, P. and Tosques, F. (2005), "Google Web APIs - An Instrument for Webometric Analyses?," *Proceedings of the 10th International Conference of the International Society for Scientometrics and Informetrics,* Stockholm (Sweden), accessed July 28, 2007 <http://www.ib.hu-berlin.de/~mayr/arbeiten/ISSI2005_Mayr_Toques.pdf>.

Mayr, P. and Walter, A.-K. (2006), "Abdeckung und Aktualität des Suchdienstes Google Scholar," *Information - Wissenschaft & Praxis,* Vol. 57 No. 3, pp.133-140, accessed July 28, 2007 <http://www.ib.hu-berlin.de/~mayr/arbeiten/IWP_3_ 06_ MayrWalter.pdf >.

Noruzi, A. (2005), "Google Scholar: The Next Generation of Citation Indexes," *Libri,* Vol. 55, pp. 170-180.

Payne, D. (2004), "Google Scholar welcomed," *The Scientist,* Vol. 5 No. 1, p.20041123-01, accessed July 28, 2007 <http://www.the-scientist.com>.

Price, G. (2004), "Google Scholar Documentation and Large PDF Files," *SearchEngineWatch,* accessed July 28, 2007 <http://blog.searchenginewatch.com/blog/041201-105511>.

Sullivan, D. (2004), "Google Scholar Offers Access To Academic Information," *Searchenginewatch,* accessed July 28, 2007 <http://searchenginewatch.com/showPage.html?page=3437471>.

Swan, A. and Brown, S. (2005), "Open access self-archiving: An author study," *Joint Information Systems Committee (JISC),* accessed July 28, 2007 <http://eprints.ecs.soton.ac.uk/10999/>.

Terdiman, D. (2004), "A Tool for Scholars Who Like to Dig Deep," *The New York Times,* Section Technology, published November 25, 2004, G6.

Changes at Google Scholar:
A Conversation with Anurag Acharya

Barbara Quint

In its own quiet way, Google Scholar has become a major force in scholarly communication. For many researchers, faculty, and students, it is the first search tool used, challenging the popularity and utility of veteran databases licensed–often at considerable cost–by academic and corporate libraries. Yet announcements about changes in the constantly evolving service seem to occur rarely and with little ballyhoo. For example, did you know that Google Scholar has launched its own digitization project, separate from the high-profile Google Book Search mass digitization? Or what about the new Key Author feature? Or the expansion into non-English languages and non-U.S./Western European content? A conversation with Anurag Acharya, the designer and missionary behind Google Scholar, helped us catch up on the latest developments.

As to how much content Google Scholar now reaches, Acharya couldn't say, beyond the understatement, "pretty large." However, he described the growth in the volume of users as exponential. Arrangements with major content providers continue to expand Google Scholar's reach. Acharya mentioned that Google was just completing the indexing of Elsevier's Science Direct collection, with several new publishers on the horizon.

He was very excited about the outreach now underway into many new languages. "We have significant coverage in Chinese, German, French, Portuguese, Spanish, Japanese, and soon Korean." In working with these languages, Google Scholar will provide translated links across languages. In traditional databases, common subject terms or descriptors may provide the primary topical linking between foreign-language and English-language content. However, in Google Scholar, the linking involves Google's translation capabilities. Acharya described the locating of related articles as "working surprisingly well." Overall, he said that non-English content lets users "find work they would never ever come close to" without Google Scholar.

Representing another effort to reach currently inaccessible content, Google Scholar now has its own digitization program. "It's a small program," said Acharya. "We mainly look for journals that would otherwise never get digitized. Under our proposal, we will digitize and host journal articles with the provision that they must be openly reachable in collaboration with publishers, fully downloadable, and fully readable. Once you get out of the U.S. and Western European space into the rest of the world, the opportunities to get and digitize research are very limited. They are often grateful for the help. It gives us the opportunity to get that country's material or make that scholarly society more visible."

I asked Acharya whether this program meant that publishers lost copyright and related revenue. He said that most of the publishers that this program might reach had "no significant opportunity to get their journals digitized or get large revenue. Basically their journals would just sit on shelves forever. We let the publishers choose what they like on dates or whatever. We're not pushing anything."

No one could ever call Acharya's approach pushy. In fact, besides his occasional public appearances at conferences, this NewsBreak may represent the main public announcement of the existence of the Google Scholar digitization effort. No press release appeared describing the service. By the way, although Acharya described the service in terms of outreach to other countries and other languages, he assured me that Google is "happy to work with anyone interested." In fact, the company is currently in negotiations with a Canadian scholarly society. Acharya said that content from the new digitization program should start entering Google Scholar before the end of the year.

However, a great many scholarly publications digitized by Google will not enter Google Scholar. Google Book Search has masses of back issues of journals digitized, as the bound volumes of periodicals come into the program from the stacks of its library partners. However, the metadata that Google Scholar needs to identify specific articles in specific issues does not exist and, at least for now, Acharya has no plans to create it. Searchers will have to remember to make a second search in Google Books, particularly for older journal content. However, scholarly book citations from Google Book Search do sometimes appear in Google Scholar search results.

Not only does Google Scholar continue to expand its content, but also its search features. A few months back, according to Acharya, it added Key Author listings to the left of search results pages. The listings are computed dynamically and have to adjust to different conventions in different fields, that is, to identify the primary author names for different types of journals in different fields of study. Acharya had another tip. Enter the name of an author as your search query to find that author's key co-authors. Acharya described the new feature as an attempt to solve the "basic fundamental problem of not knowing where the query wants to go. We need to take you beyond the query. Sometimes the Key Author feature works shockingly well." He found it especially useful in tracking new scholarly developments where new terminology emerged to describe a phenomenon after the original research. Using the Key Author feature, you can reach back to the original research. Using the "Related Articles" posted under each search result is another method.

As for the future, we'll just have to watch and wait–and keep in touch with Anurag Acharya.

Attitudes of OhioLINK Librarians Toward Google Scholar

Joan Giglierano

INTRODUCTION

Since Google Scholar's introduction as a beta site in November 2004, academic librarians have been debating what to do with it. Here was a tool with the Google cachet, guaranteed to mesmerize users, from undergraduate to faculty researchers, with its claim to easily and quickly locate scholarly resources in that inimitable, painless, Googly way. It even threw in "cited by" references! Could this innovation supplant the expensive subscription databases purchased with libraries' ever-shrinking budgets, or would it prove to be lacking in significant enough ways to be easily dismissed as an alternative for locating peer-reviewed articles?

Almost three years after Google Scholar's inception, only a third of Ohio Library and Information Network (OhioLINK) member libraries link to it from their Web sites. This article reports the results of a survey conducted during July 2007 to find out:

- What enters into OhioLINK libraries' decisions about whether or not to promote Google Scholar to their users?
- Where on their Web sites do OhioLINK libraries choose to place Google Scholar links?
- Are OhioLINK libraries incorporating Google Scholar into their instruction classes, and how do they position it with subscription databases?

This article will present the survey responses, using them to summarize OhioLINK libraries' approaches to Google Scholar and comparing them with other research findings. It will conclude with recommendations for libraries still undecided about whether to embrace (or even to shake hands) with Google Scholar.

ABOUT OhioLINK

The OhioLINK consortium, in operation since 1992, has grown to include most of the academic libraries in Ohio, as well as the state library and a growing number of public libraries. Member libraries have benefited from the consortium's combined buying power, which enabled them to provide their users with access to hundreds of databases, thousands of e-journals, and other electronic resources.[1] Member libraries often link directly to the OhioLINK list of databases for their descriptions, rather than writing their own. Through committees such as Reference and User Services (USC) and Cooperative Information Resources Management (CIRM), libraries exchange information about new databases and other products purchased cooperatively, and other issues affecting the membership.

OhioLINK reported sharing link resolver information with Google, in order to implement Google Scholar, at the USC meeting on May 16, 2005. Once implemented, links leading to resources purchased by OhioLINK, such as centrally purchased full-text e-journal articles, would be displayed automatically for on-campus users, though branch or off-campus users would need to add OhioLINK to their Scholar Preferences.[2] The network administrator informed member institutions of advantages to submitting their individual link resolver information directly to Google, as suggested on the Google Scholar site: "We strongly encourage you to provide your patrons' IP address ranges. Many good services go unused simply because people don't configure their preferences to utilize them,"[3] though only one library in the OhioLINK consortium, Ohio State University, has done so.[4] These "Find it with OLinks" links follow the name of the article. Resources with a match in the OhioLINK central catalog include links labeled "OhioLINK OLinks." Though OhioLINK did not opt to promote or link to Google Scholar from its Web site, it issued a news item about Google Scholar in May 2005, telling users about the links and how to set up Scholar Preferences for off-campus access to linked resources.[5]

METHODOLOGY

In July 2007, the author examined Web sites of all OhioLINK academic libraries to find out if they included links to Google Scholar. Each school's name, the URL of its library's home page, and the names and URLs of pages on its site where Google Scholar links appeared were logged on a spreadsheet. Concurrently, the author created a brief survey using SurveyMonkey software, and then posted requests for responses on the general OhioLINK listserv and also on its Reference and User Services listserv. The survey was open for responses during the entire month. Information that could identify an individual or institution was not requested, and IP address information was blocked, to assure anonymity.

PRESENCE OF LINKS TO GOOGLE SCHOLAR ON OhioLINK ACADEMIC LIBRARY WEB SITES

Of 80 OhioLINK academic library Web sites examined,[6] 26, or 32% included at least one link to Google Scholar; 54, or 68% had no links to Google Scholar. Bowling Green State University had the most Google Scholar links (11), followed by the College of Wooster and the University of Cincinnati (10 each), and Baldwin-Wallace College and Ohio State University (8 each). The libraries linking to Google Scholar were evenly split between public institutions and private universities or colleges, with 13 each. Twenty-four were libraries at 4-year schools and two were at 2-year schools. Of the 54 OhioLINK library Web sites without links to Google Scholar, 33 were at private institutions and 21 were at public. Thirty-four of the non-linking libraries were at 4-year institutions, nineteen were at 2-year schools, and one was at a professional campus.

SURVEY RESULTS

The survey received 50 responses. The majority (32, or 64.0%) said their libraries' sites did not link to Google Scholar. The most frequent reason given for not doing so was wanting students to use the databases the library had paid for; if the library provided a link to Google Scholar, students might not use anything else. Many expressed concern over the quality of Google Scholar results, mentioning too many hits, lack of information about the sources it pulls from, and the age of the articles it retrieves. Several respondents cited lack of promotion of Google Scholar by OhioLINK; not knowing enough about Google Scholar; or not having enough time to investigate it in order to make the decision to link to it. Others said they link to Google, but not to Google Scholar, on their Web sites, while a few stated they do not like or trust Google. Other reasons given were: fear of confusing students; desire to avoid frustrating users who thought they had to pay for resources Google Scholar retrieved; concern that links to OhioLINK and local full-text resources were not comprehensive; lack of awareness of Google Scholar on their campuses; and faculty who do not want students to use Google or Internet resources.

Eighteen responses (38.0%) said their libraries' sites linked to Google Scholar. Six libraries (33.3%) reported links from the library home page, with an equal number reporting links on an Internet resources page or search engines list. Fewer reported links from an alphabetical or a subject databases list (5, or 27.8%, for each). The greatest number of libraries with links to Google Scholar (10, or 55.6%) placed them elsewhere, such as on a "Research Resources" or a "Find Articles and Journals" page, or on a separate "Google Scholar" or "Google for Researchers" page.

The survey revealed far more exclusion than inclusion of Google Scholar in instruction classes on both the undergraduate and graduate levels. Twenty-eight responses (58.3%) said librarians on their campuses did not routinely mention Google Scholar in undergraduate instruction classes; 11 (22.9%) said they did; and 9 (18.8%) did not know. When asked if instruction librarians at their library routinely mentioned Google Scholar in graduate instruction classes, 30 responses (62.5%) said no; 9

(18.8%) said yes; and 9 (18.8%) said they did not know. The negative responses to this question included 11 self-identified as institutions that did not offer graduate classes (in retrospect, this question should have included "not applicable" as a choice), but even taking that into consideration, it is evident that most responding libraries do not include Google Scholar in graduate instruction classes.

The most frequently given reasons for not routinely telling undergraduates about Google Scholar in instruction classes were time constraints; wanting students to use library databases; quality of results; and lack of information about what is being searched by Google Scholar. Other reasons given were redundancy (it duplicates other resources); reluctance of faculty to let students use Google (and, by extension, Scholar); believing it more appropriate for graduate students; and lack of knowledge about Google Scholar. A few individuals said they, personally, mention it to undergraduate classes, even though most other librarians at their institution do not, and others said they tell students about it when working with them one-on-one, though they don't teach it in instruction classes. Several said though they do not routinely do so, they occasionally tell classes about Google Scholar, and some said they mention it, but only to warn students about its limitations. One respondent said he/she planned to start telling both undergraduate and graduate instruction classes about it, since receiving directions about setting up links from Google Scholar to OhioLINK resources. Reasons given for omitting mention of Google Scholar in graduate classes were similar, though less varied.

HOW OhioLINK LIBRARIANS ARE USING GOOGLE SCHOLAR

A few survey responses, such as the following, expressed enthusiasm for Google Scholar:

> We love Google Scholar and love the OLinks option. It has been helpful in allowing students to access materials in random databases that they may not have searched on their own.

> Researchers are using Google Scholar more and more to upload their research and publishers are putting more information into Google Scholar. It has become one of the key resources for scholarly research. Also, our full-text journals link there.

As Google Scholar integrates with OhioLINK access to the full-text of items, it serves the dual purpose of getting to reputable journal literature while allowing students to use the Google interface. I always suggest to my classes that if they need to use the Web to locate research articles, use Google Scholar and not just Google. Plus, sometimes the only way I can locate certain items easily is via Google Scholar. It's a good complement to OhioLINK's databases.

Several librarians said they used Google Scholar when answering reference questions and when doing their own research, as well as steering individual students and faculty to it when appropriate:

> We do not actively promote it but consider it an important tool. We provide the link in several places and frequently demonstrate setting up preferences for students doing higher levels of academic research.

> Some of the librarians here promote Google Scholar at the reference desk, but usually after using another 1 or 2 databases first. The reason for this has been that if you just show them only Google Scholar they tend to not use the other databases and miss some good info; if you demonstrate it and promote it after using a couple of other databases, it shows more accurately how it complements the databases and they're more likely to do a more comprehensive search.

A number of librarians approached the question of Google Scholar pragmatically, recognizing the likelihood that students were aware of it, and wanting to help them optimize its use:

> Students already use Google. By directing them to Google Scholar, potentially they will find more appropriate resources than by searching Google only. We don't feel that we are promoting Google Scholar; rather, we are showing students (and faculty) how to enhance its usefulness by linking to OhioLINK for location information.

> Some librarians here address it, some ignore it. There is not a formal policy to ignore it. I choose to address it in many of my sessions because (1) it is in many instances a useful resource, and (2) ignoring it is akin to burying your head in the sand while the

tide is rising–users are highly aware of it, using it, and we look silly when we pretend it's not there. Like it or not, it is part of the conversation.

WHY OhioLINK LIBRARIANS DO NOT PUBLICIZE GOOGLE SCHOLAR

Based on comments from the survey responses, OhioLINK librarians want to train students to start their research with resources on their library's Web site, not with Google or, by extension, Google Scholar.

We wish to emphasize the research databases available through the library. It is a major task to draw students' attention away from Google as it is.

[We are] loath to direct students to anything other than our databases since our fight is to get them away from simply searching Google.

Our students would use only Google Scholar if that's what we mentioned and indicated it's o.k. to go there

The comparative "quality and ease of use" and "versatility and access" of subscription databases, as well as the desire to promote the use of these resources the library has invested in, were other reasons given for not publicizing Google Scholar:

I believe many of my colleagues shun the use of Google Scholar because they feel that they should be the direct pipeline to scholarly resources and that students won't get good results if they try to use Google Scholar on their own. In many cases I think the instinct to react negatively to a tool like Google Scholar grows from a self protection mechanism, not a sense of arrogance about one's knowledge, although some small percentage of colleagues probably think that they are too expert to use it. I showed it to a professor from another institution the other day who was doing a high-powered research project and he was thrilled!

What does a student need with 176,000 hits that refer back to OLinks? If we are paying for GOOD information, let's teach how to find it and not confuse students with Google "Scholar."

I believe there are still many misleading results from a Google Scholar search. On the other hand, I just used it successfully with a student Monday night–but I was there to help interpret things for her. Otherwise she would have wasted a great deal of time. She had never heard of it.

We use [Google Scholar] sometimes in helping students do research, but we do not do any promoting of it. We still find that [Google Scholar] is still weak in providing current articles and information.

Many librarians clearly feel they have no time to learn yet another tool, and perceive Google Scholar as offering nothing new to their users. Several mentioned how difficult it is already to cover use of the library catalog, the OhioLINK catalog, and subscription databases in instruction classes, without adding yet another topic or resource to the mix.

MISCONCEPTIONS ABOUT GOOGLE SCHOLAR

The concerns about Google Scholar expressed by OhioLINK librarians in their survey responses echoed shortcomings discussed early on by authors such as Jacsó, Myhill, Gardner and Eng, Abram, Kesselman, O'Leary, and Wlekinski.[7] Since several years have passed since these early studies were done, some perceptions librarians have based on these articles may need to be revisited. For example, a reason given for reluctance to link to Google Scholar was the fear that users would be upset if they were asked to pay for full-text resources that show up in Google Scholar search results. A way to avoid this situation is for academic libraries in Ohio to teach users to recognize the "Find it with OLinks" links as a way to online full text, and instruct them to set up Google Scholar Preferences to enable these links off-campus. Some OhioLINK libraries, such as Wright State University and Ohio State University,[8] include information on their sites explaining to their affiliated users what to do if prompted to pay, and how to avoid payment requests by choosing the OLinks or using interlibrary loan.

Another perception expressed in responses to this survey was Google Scholar's inferiority to library databases, for exmaple, its results were "not as 'good'," it was "less user-friendly," it "does not access nearly enough sites to ensure good research results." Yet studies show Google Scholar returning as good or better results in some cases, for example, when searching interdisciplinary topics and for gray literature, and for seminal works on given topics.[9] Neuhaus et al. found considerable overlap between Google Scholar and library databases in science, medicine, and engineering, with less in social sciences and humanities.[10] Lack of duplication with library database results does not necessarily mean Google Scholar's results are worse, just different, and underscores the value of using Google Scholar as an adjunct when seeking to do a comprehensive search. Google Scholar's results display can be confusing, with its mixture of articles, technical reports, conference papers, books, dissertations, Web sites, and other resources, as well as multiple versions of publications, all presented together. Standard library databases such as ERIC, PsycINFO, and MLA Bibliography mix resources of different types together in their results, too; while they offer limit options that allow searchers to filter out unwanted resource types, these limiters are seldom intuitive to novice searchers. Users of Google Scholar benefit from instruction, as users of library databases do, to fully understand conventions and capabilities of the tool.[11]

COMPARISON WITH OTHER SURVEY RESULTS

In the few years since Google Scholar's introduction, other surveys of librarians and examinations of library Web sites have been done and reported in the literature. Mullen and Hartman studied 113 Association of Research Libraries (ARL) university members' Web sites in 2005 and found 6 libraries, or 5% of their sample, with links to Google Scholar on their homepages; 27 (24%) had Google Scholar links on their lists of alphabetical databases; 16 (14%) had links on their subject databases pages; 14 (12.5%) included Google Scholar links in subject guides; and 22 institutions (19.5%) listed Google Scholar as a search engine or Internet search tool. Two ARL institutions placed the Google Scholar search box directly on their home pages, in contrast to none of the OhioLINK libraries. Six ARL libraries (5%) cataloged Google Scholar in their OPACs, in contrast to 2 (2%) of the OhioLINK libraries.[12] Meltzer asked University of California librarians about their use of Google Scholar in 2005, and the comments she received were quite similar to those of the OhioLINK librarians, two years later. She found a "core of respondents do not use Google Scholar at all," as well as others who found Google Scholar useful for "getting at older, more obscure, interdisciplinary, and difficult to locate materials quickly and simply . . . sometimes easier to use than traditional resources. It provides another point of entry to the world of scholarship . . . [when] used as an entrée into the use of OpenURL or licensed resources, and as an option for non-UC affiliated users."[13] York examined 9 library Web sites, finding a range of tone "from wildly defensive to surprisingly embracive" in their presentations of Google Scholar.[14] He also summarized the concerns of librarians about Google Scholar, many of which were repeated in OhioLINK librarians' survey responses:

> First, users will abandon library databases and the library catalog as they come to use Google Scholar exclusively for their research, a concern that seems to be most often addressed by providing copious links to library databases and billing Scholar as incomplete and redundant, while library databases are sophisticated, comprehensive, and reliable.

> Second, users will come to think of librarians as irrelevant now that they have easy access to a powerful and simple (if deceptive) tool like Google Scholar; the typical solution to prevent this erosion is to provide numerous links and pointers to "Ask a Librarian."

> Third is the fear that users will be led astray into a world of incomplete and redundant content that will water down scholarship and dilute the quality of academic work. Unable to distinguish quality sources from those of a lower grade, users will become simple and unsophisticated as they become accustomed to using only that single, clean, tempting search box. The most common approach to this concern is to point out how many advanced narrowing and filtering options the library databases have.

> Finally, libraries appear to be greatly concerned that users will be tricked into paying for content the library already subscribes to.[15]

The Urban Libraries Council reported results of a survey done in July 2005 that received 54 responses. A much higher percentage of respondents to this survey (96%) did not link to Google Scholar from their Web sites or pathfinders, compared to 64% of the OhioLINK survey respondents, and 98% had no plans to offer staff or patron instruction on Google Scholar, compared to the 22.9% of OhioLINK libraries that include Google Scholar in undergraduate instruction classes and the 18.8% that include it in graduate instruction classes.[16]

RECOMMENDATIONS

The results of the survey and examination of OhioLINK academic libraries' Web sites reported in this article show that, while in the minority, a number of institutions are finding enough merit in Google Scholar to link to it from their sites. While relatively few libraries routinely mention Google Scholar during instruction classes, comments indicate librarians are telling users about it in one-to-one consultations, and using it themselves as another tool for answering reference questions.

Google Scholar is not a panacea, but it can be a very useful complement to library databases, especially with the links to full text and the OhioLINK catalog displayed in search results. Many OhioLINK member libraries take their cues from OhioLINK on promoting databases and other resources. While OhioLINK may not see fit to put a Google Scholar search box or even to include a link to Google Scholar on its own Web site, member libraries already familiar with Google Scholar's strengths as well as its limitations could help other librarians understand them. Suggestions for best practices for Web placement and presenting Google Scholar to students and faculty might also be disseminated through OhioLINK for the benefit of the many librarians with no time to find out about this tool on their own. Perhaps OhioLINK and Ohio State, the only library in the consortium that has separately provided its IP ranges to Google, might document the benefits of individual libraries' doing so, such as more exposure of local e-resources and individual library branding, and provide technical guidance to expedite the process.

The organizational culture has a definite bearing on whether librarians feel comfortable discussing Google Scholar in an instruction class, or if they prefer to introduce it to users on a case-by-case basis. In making decisions about if and how to tell users about Google Scholar, a sensible approach is to treat it as another tool, with strengths and weaknesses like any other. Introducing library databases first, then following with Google Scholar, is an instruction technique that works well for some librarians.[17] Others use the authenticated links in Google Scholar and the magic words "free full-text articles" to get students' attention, then introduce specialized subscription databases; some even have students compare and contrast content retrieved by each.[18]

Using the "cited by" feature in Google Scholar search results to teach the concept of forward citation searching can be a much simpler way to get this concept across to students than using the ISI Web of Science, and is especially valuable for those libraries not able to afford the ISI product.[19] As Cathcart and Roberts wrote, "Because it offers the familiarity of Google, yet introduces the user to scholarly articles and the concept of a citation index, it could serve as a bridge to the more reliable, comprehensive resources offered by libraries."[20] Teaching good information literacy skills enables students to judge the quality of results retrieved through Google Scholar, as they do when using subscription databases, even if there is no academic journals filter available to help.

For graduate students and faculty, Google Scholar increases comprehensiveness of search results through its prowess at finding gray literature and materials in Web-based institutional repositories, among other valuable resources. As Jeffrey Pomerantz wrote, "Given that library users are using Google Scholar, it is to libraries' benefit to see that it is used well."[21] Google Scholar presents real opportunities for libraries to help their users get to resources already bought, as well as to other valuable content freely available on the Web, and should not be ignored.

NOTES

1. OhioLINK, "The Ohio Library and Information Network," OhioLINK, <http://www.ohiolink.edu/about/what-is-ol.html> (accessed July 20, 2007).

2. Reference and User Services Committee, Minutes, May 16, 2005, Ohio LINK, <http://silver.ohiolink.edu/minutes/usc051605.html> (accessed July 31, 2007).

3. Google, "Google Scholar Support for Libraries," Google, <http://scholar.google.com/intl/en/scholar/libraries.html> (accessed July 31, 2007).

4. Thomas Dowling, OhioLINK, e-mail communication to the author, August 21, 2006.

5. OhioLINK, "Using Google Scholar? Look for OLinks!" May 23, 2005, OhioLINK, <http://olc7.ohiolink.edu/whatsnew/archives/2005_05.html> (accessed August 1, 2007).

6. Branch campus libraries were not counted separately from their main campus locations.

7. Péter Jacsó, "Google Scholar: The Pros and the Cons," *Online Information Review*, v.29 no.2 (February 2005): 208-214; Péter Jacsó, "Google Scholar Beta," Thomson Gale, <http://www.gale.com/servlet/HTMLFileServlet?imprint=9999& region=7&fileName=/reference/archive/200412/googlescholar.html> (accessed February 9, 2006); Martin Myhill, "Google Scholar," *The Charleston Advisor*, v.6 no.4 (April 2005): 49-52; Susan Gardner and Susanna Eng, "Gaga Over Google? Scholar in the Social Sciences," *Library Hi Tech News*, v.22 no.8 (2005): 42-45; Stephen Abram, "Google Scholar: Thin Edge of the Wedge?" *Information Outlook*, v.9 no.1 (January 2005): 44-46; Martin Kesselman and Sarah Barbara Watstein, "Google Scholar and Libraries: Point/Counterpoint," *Reference Services Review*, v.33 no.4 (2005): 380-387; Mick O'Leary, "Google Scholar: What's in it for You?" Information Today v.22 no.7 (July/August 2005): 35-39; Joann M.Wleklinski, "Studying Google Scholar: Wall to Wall Coverage?" *Online*, v.29 no.3 (May/June 2005): 22-26.

8. Wright State University Libraries, "Using Google Scholar at the WSU Libraries," Wright State University, <http://www.libraries.wright.edu/find/reference/

gscholar.html> (accessed July 19, 2007); The Ohio State University Libraries, "Google Scholar," The Ohio State University, <http://library.ohio-state.edu/record=e1000511> (accessed July 19, 2007); The Ohio State University Libraries, "Making Google Scholar Work for You," The Ohio State University, <http://library.osu.edu/sites/it/ER/GoogleScholar/FAQ.php> (accessed July 19, 2007).

9. Janice Adlington and Chris Benda, "Checking Under the Hood: Evaluating Google Scholar for Reference Use," in *Libraries and Google*, ed. by William Miller and Rita M. Pellen (Binghamton, NY: The Haworth Press, Inc., 2005), 146; Rena Helms-Park, Pavlina Radia, and Paul Stapleton, "A Preliminary Assessment of Google Scholar as a Source of EAP Students' Research Materials," *Internet & Higher Education*, v.10 no.1 (January 2007), 65-76; Robert Schroeder, "Pointing Users Toward Citation Searching: Using Google Scholar and Web of Science," *portal: Libraries & the Academy*, v.7 no.2 (April, 2007): 243-248; Ellen Meltzer, "UC [University of California] Libraries Use of Google Scholar," California Digital Library, <http://www.cdlib.org/inside/assess/evaluation_activities/docs/2005/googleScholar_summary_0805.pdf> (accessed September 12, 2006).

10. Chris Neuhaus, Ellen Neuhaus, Alan Asher, and Clint Wrede, "The Depth and Breadth of Google Scholar: An Empirical Study," *portal: Libraries & the Academy*, v.6 no.2 (April 2006): 127-141.

11. Glenn Haya, Else Nygren, and Wilhelm Widmark, "Metalib and Google Scholar: A User Study," *Online Information Review*, v.31 no.3 (2007): 365-375.

12. Laura Bowering Mullen and Karen A. Hartman, "Google Scholar and the Library Web Site: The Early Response by ARL Libraries," *College & Research Libraries*, v.67 no.2 (March 2006): 106-122.

13. Meltzer, 1.

14. Maurice C. York, "Calling the Scholars Home: Google Scholar as a Tool for Rediscovering the Academic Library," in *Libraries and Google*, ed. by William Miller and Rita M. Pellen (Binghamton, NY: The Haworth Press, Inc., 2005), 119.

15. York, 124, formatting added.

16. Urban Libraries Council, "Google Scholar Survey Results," Urban Libraries Council, <http://www.urbanlibraries.org/july2005-googlescholar.html> (accessed July 30, 2007).

17. Information Literacy (ili-l) Listserv Archives, "Google Scholar and Bibliographic Instruction [thread]," American Library Association, <http://lists.ala.org/wws/arc/ili-l/2007-02/msg00074.html> (accessed February 21, 2007).

18. Cheryl LaGuardia, "Connecting with Researchers, or, Will You Have Google with That Search?" Library Journal E-Views Blog, <http://www.libraryjournal.com/blog/1100000310/post/1460012346.html> (accessed August 2, 2007); Information Literacy (ili-l) Listserv Archives, "Google Scholar and Bibliographic Instruction [thread]."

19. Schroeder, 245.

20. Rachael Cathcart and Amanda Roberts, "Evaluating Google Scholar as a Tool for Information Literacy," in *Libraries and Google*, ed. by William Miller and Rita M. Pellen (Binghamton, NY: The Haworth Press, Inc., 2005), 175.

21. Pomerantz, Jeffrey, "Google Scholar and 100 Percent Availability of Information," *Information Technology & Libraries*, v.25 no.2 (June 2006): 52-56.

Using Google Scholar
at the Reference Desk

Karen Bronshteyn
Kathryn Tvaruzka

INTRODUCTION

Students and faculty have discovered Google Scholar (GS), even at institutions where its use is not at all promoted by the library, and where it may even be ignored by reference staff. It is possible that GS is not used frequently at the reference desk for many reasons, including distrust of the search returns; the lack of functionality in comparison to what one is accustomed to in a scholarly database search interface; the belief that during a teachable moment such as the reference transaction one should use library databases; and fear that people will not look at librarians as relevant or professional if they resort to a publicly available resource.

A survey of eight California campus libraries found that "a core of respondents do not use Google Scholar at all. Others use it rarely, instead strongly preferring licensed article databases purchased by the libraries for use in specific disciplines. Some are reluctant to use it because they are unsure of what it actually covers."[1] In addition to legitimate concerns about the search limitations and exuberant results of Google Scholar, librarians are known to respond negatively to students' over- reliance on Google.[2] This causes a professional dilemma–do we ignore Google products at the reference desk, relying solely on the products that we trust and are skilled at using (hoping the student will pick up on our technique), or do we acknowledge the popularity and simplicity of Google and demonstrate the most effective search techniques for Google Scholar?

While librarians will do their best to direct researchers to scholarly databases, an argument must be made that we at least acknowledge Google Scholar–its pros and the cons–in order to teach appropriate searching strategies to students and researchers. This study attempts to identify the most common instances when GS may assist in a reference transaction, and includes as examples reference questions that benefited from GS. As any transaction at the reference desk serves as a teachable moment, techniques for one-on-one instruction on GS are also described. Additionally, it advocates attentiveness to campus-wide training needs in GS searching.

WHEN TO USE GOOGLE SCHOLAR AT THE REFERENCE DESK

At least five reasons are noteworthy:

1. To complete a citation and to find the full text.
2. To identify portions of monographs (using a full-text search), or to relocate something found earlier.
3. To locate an item that the library doesn't own.
4. To locate items when library databases/catalogs are down or not functioning properly (if the library participates in Open WorldCat).
5. To conduct interdisciplinary metasearching for suggestion of another database.

The following illustrations of utility include a few examples of reference desk transactions at the University of Wisconsin–Eau Claire (UWEC) where reference librarians used library resources first and then ultimately solved the information need using GS as a tool of last resort.

To Complete a Citation and to Find the Full Text

This is a point-of-need reference transaction for full-text retrieval when the citation is supplied in complete or incomplete form, and/or when the full text is not available via library databases. This is sometimes an obscure item, and the student is often discouraged by the amount of time already spent on its pursuit.

Example: A student needed to identify/complete a citation and find the full text of an article published within the last few years entitled "Positive health . . ." by author Carol Ryff. We tried a federated search through eight biology/science databases and found a good match in Biological Abstracts.

The full text not being available, the interlibrary loan option appeared, but, of course, the assignment was due the next morning. An advanced search in GS ("positive health" as exact phrase and Ryff in the author field) yielded a few results including a promising group of eight called "Positive health: connecting well-being with biology," in *Philosophical Transactions of the Royal Society B*. Of this group of eight, only two links went through to the full text; one was clearly from the journal publisher, and the other was reposted PDF content on an .edu site.

At first glance the publisher site appeared to charge a fee to download; however, there was a PDF link which was active, and the copyright date matched the student's description. The other links included a publication catalog entry, a broken link, a Pubmed citation, and error messages from Ingenta saying that journals from the Royal Society are no longer hosted. The student was happy to walk away with a printout of the PDF from the publisher's site, but due to the complicated mix of results, it is not clear if she could replicate the search.

To Use Full-Text Search Capabilities
to Identify Portions of Monographs

On several occasions at the UWEC reference desk, students were hoping to reconnect with a source found earlier or with one mentioned in class by a professor. Some of the sources were found via Google Scholar using a full-text search.

Example: In one particular instance, a student with a photocopy of a book chapter had trouble quoting it precisely, because of an illegible word. While our library did own this particular title, all copies of that edition were checked out. We performed a Google Scholar search on the chapter title, "Gendered Media: The Influence of Media on Views of Gender," to see if it was available online. It was available, and was clearly a scanned copy, the quality of which matched her "photocopy" exactly. Since she received the copy from her professor, one can infer that her professor accessed the same scanned copy, possibly obtained via GS. But here is a perfect case in point of a request turning into a teachable moment, as the student had additional sources to retrieve for the course, which allowed for a slower walk-through of GS advanced searching. As our library catalog has limited table of contents-enriched records, this demonstration served to benefit the student for additional book chapter searches.

To Locate an Item That the Library Doesn't Own

A student does not need to remember "WorldCat" for a widened library book search, if enough area libraries are participating in Open WorldCat. But they are able to remember *Google*–and their zip code. This may be enough to make a proximal connection with a source. Furthermore, despite our best efforts to incorporate important publicly available online sources into our library catalog, we don't fling our net as wide as Google's. As with the other above examples of utility, GS can also be used as a tool of last resort to track down local resources.

Example: The UWEC library catalog showed that we had access to just one special issue of *Wisconsin Medical Journal* in print, whereas our periodicals list and SFX menu showed nothing owned. A GS search, however, found over 500 relevant matches in full-text PDF through the Wisconsin Medical Society. The results were in ranked order with the ability to resort by date. This being part of an answer to an e-mail question, the response was sent with a hotlink to the source. No explanation of how to use GS was sent, although a link to a standard *how-to* posting would provide students with additional information, and is worth further consideration.

To Locate Items When Library Databases/Catalogs Are Down or Not Functioning Properly

Google and Google Scholar have helped at UWEC when the system-wide "Universal Borrowing" catalog did not work. (It is also useful to note that not all UWEC library catalog users know to switch to "Other Catalogs–All Universal Borrowing Libraries" to locate an item. GS simplifies this by adding the link "UWEC Library–FindIt!") Limited testing on the reference desk with GS versus Google led more directly to results indicating ownership at system libraries. The University of California Libraries report also mentions using GS in this manner, in particular, when their link resolver is down, or to save time in completing the citation linker form.[3]

To Suggest an Alternative (and Possibly Better) Database

Because GS searches a variety of interdisciplinary databases, its scope has the potential to extend beyond federated search engines customized by discipline. Using GS after a search with a subscription federated search tool, or even after conducting sophisticated searches in two or more discipline-specific databases, may serve to identify an additional database possibility. The success of this strategy was previously discussed by reference librarians at Florida Gulf Coast University testing GS. After searching ProQuest and Lexis/Nexis without satisfaction, an exact phrase search in GS identified relevant results in Wilson OmniFile.[4]

To Find Additional Scholarly Resources or Supplemental Materials

There are several additional instances of utility that are worth considering, such as a need to include gray literature, conference papers, and proceedings in a search; a need to conduct cited reference searching that extends beyond the functionality or availability of subscription databases; to export citations; or instances where relevancy ranking is of particular benefit, such as assistance in identifying seminal articles. Google Scholar may also be useful when a student is terribly confused about publication formats, and in some cases the results may serve to lead the student back to more traditional library resources.

Example: A student was looking for "a source," with the fuzzy conception that it was a monograph owned at UWEC, by the title of *Health Care Workers Role Conceptions*. A library catalog search yielded no results. A Google Scholar search led to the Pubmed citation of "Health care workers' role conceptions and orientation to family-centered child care," an article in *Nursing Research*, 1979. The student nodded in agreement–all of those extra words sounded very familiar, as did the journal title (although she didn't know it was a journal), and the date. The GS search did not yield the full text, but it saved the step of looking up the source using the SFX (link resolver) menu, since the results stated UWEC LIBRARY–FULL TEXT. The full text, in this occasion, was microfilm. This being the only source the student needed, our discussion switched from Google Scholar to an explanation of journals and periodicals, how to locate microfilm, and how to receive help in the periodicals department.

DEMONSTRATING TECHNIQUE FOR SEARCHING GOOGLE SCHOLAR

Unlike a library instruction session, the moments spent in reference transactions are requested by a student who is engaged in the discovery. It is a teachable moment, one we can capitalize on, where we should promote effective search techniques and source evaluation. Students may already be avid Google users, but they often are novices at searching specifically for "scholarly" resources, and their evolving understanding of this term is complimented by one-on-one instruction with a simplified interface lacking distracting notations and (seemingly) excessive drop-down menus and search boxes.

While acknowledging the popularity of Google's simple interface, librarians can use the opportunity to explain the additional functionality available in GS and the even greater functionality available in subscription database XYZ. This also provides an opportunity for stressing the need to use a variety of access points and for evaluating sources.

There are a number of techniques that extend beyond the realm of what Google searchers are used to, and they offer time-saving search precision.

Advanced search. Although Google searchers may occasionally use the advanced search screen, they may not be expecting a difference in functionality with GS. In addition to the familiar exact phrase search feature and Boolean limits, GS offers the ability to limit by author or publication name (using variations of spelling/abbreviation,) or limiting to a subject area (a predetermined group of academic disciplines). There is also a date limit, but unfortunately, it is not consistent.

Results groupings. Results are grouped and the groups are ranked. Within each group there may be a variety of editions of the work, and some of them may be accessible and others not. Students need to be instructed to click on the notation "all X versions" to obtain the greatest odds in accessing a document.

Quick links to additional sources. A great value-added function is the "Cited by" link below a search result. Several highly esteemed subscription databases still do not have this feature. This link and others, such as "Related Articles" may not be noticed unless pointed out to users.

Scholar preferences. Just below the advanced search link is a preferences feature that may need to be demonstrated at the reference desk. When students return to their home computer, they can set their preference to recognize their home library and to export citations to a preferred program.

Evaluation. Using GS as a discovery tool with the user or student is a great opportunity to reiterate the necessity to evaluate one's source and to reinvestigate the meaning of "scholarly." GS results offer a springboard to additional resources that can help the student to evaluate a source, such as the "cited by" link and the identification of specialized databases. It is also an opportunity to invite them back for additional help in evaluating the sources they will find on their own.

Additionally, GS is a good resource to demonstrate in one-on-one consultations with students from online colleges who come to use the library facilities, for community users, particularly home-school families, or other users without consistent access to subscription resources, or with a limited time to learn them.

LEARNING FROM GOOGLE SCHOLAR
DEMONSTRATIONS

The introduction of GS in a reference desk transaction can be an opportunity for library staff to learn as well. For example, if your library maintains files or records for various course assignments, or in tandem with course-specific information literacy sessions, it may be advantageous to note when GS was used to track down items listed on a course reading list. This certainly will aid your colleagues when the next "deer in headlights" student arrives at the desk. Given the fear and distrust mentioned earlier, a colleague may spin her wheels with other resources or refer people to interlibrary loan without trying GS. Plus, the occasional discovery of a freely available source could result in its addition to the library catalog.

Another learning instrument is the discourse with the user. Reflect on the comments you hear during demonstrations of GS. Here are a few comments from UWEC reference desk users: "I didn't know it (GS) was separate (from Google)"; "I didn't know to click there (on *more*)"; "I didn't know about *advanced search*." The most frequent comment has been not knowing that GS is "separate" or how to get to it, even though the student's professor uses and promotes GS. This shows that some training is needed for both students and faculty, and librarians should take on that role so that we can draw comparisons to more appropriate sources and direct attention to the proper evaluation of materials.

Faculty Instruction

Faculty training does not have to be as in-depth as "train the trainer" instruction; it can simply take the form of a brief "Advanced Google Scholar" workshop. Faculty need to know how to maximize their access; therefore part of the "advanced" facet of the workshop could be using GS results to transform research strategy into identification of the most advantageous subscription database. A faculty workshop is a good opportunity to share the comments you've collected interacting with students using GS, so that they can keep in mind their referrals which may require a little bit of clarification, including the advice to promote GS usage while on the campus property (IP range) or to set a Scholar Preference to your institution, to gain the most access into subscription resources.

Student Instruction

Google search engine users are not generally anticipating the nuances and additional functionality of GS, and yet it becomes a good selling point. "The notion that Google has some esoteric, previously untapped capabilities that are particularly well-suited for work on a research project is a much easier sell"[5] [than a subscription database].

They are certainly already sold on Google and like resources. LibQUAL+ (survey) results reported in the library literature consistently document large numbers of daily Web searchers in comparison to significantly smaller numbers of daily library resource searchers. Metasearch usability studies show that students gravitate toward uncluttered quick-search interfaces and have a preference for combined searching (interdisciplinary or variety of formats). Students grow impatient with cluttered search screens and lengthy explanations for selecting a database or resource.[6]

Although a reference desk transaction may end with GS, the introduction of GS in an instruction session may be most beneficial at the beginning. Google Scholar's no-frills appearance would cut down on the "noise" affecting students' retention of information, and they would be able to focus on effective search tips and practice with an exercise in critical evaluation and identification of "scholarly." This may set the stage for a more compelling introduction to library resources. It is difficult to incorporate higher level concepts, such as source evaluation, into library instruction without a mention of popular, over-used tools. To optimize the potential for recall of lessons learned in a critical thinking exercise, students need to use a tool they recognize and will reuse on occasion. GS instruction (and comparisons to subscription databases) may also better help students understand the value of library resources.[7] In a recent usability study of Google Scholar versus Metalib, where half of the 32 users had instruction, it was found that the instruction positively impacted the students' results. (It is also worth considering that GS performed better than Metalib).[8]

Kesselman and Watstein suggest promoting flexibility:

> We have much to offer users in learning how to think critically aboutresearch tools of all kinds, in addition to the items they locate by means of those tools. . . . As part of our information literacy efforts, we must also teach our users the importance of being flexible in their research. There is no longer just one place to look for information, or one way to search. It's that simple.[9]

Librarians can practice this advice at the reference desk when we try GS at times that it might be of benefit.

CONCLUSION

Embracing all of the tools at our disposal and recognizing the popularity of Google and the affinity that novice searchers have for "easy" interfaces, some reference librarians are seizing the opportunity for a prime teachable moment at the reference desk. Google Scholar can be used at the reference desk as a type of last-resort resource, particularly for exact-citation retrieval, with occasional effective results. By using it as a last resort, the librarian expresses that in a hierarchy of scholarly resources, it belongs near the bottom. The librarian also demonstrates effective techniques for searching GS, because it can on occasion deliver longer abstracts and even some freely available full-text items from journals not included in library databases. Google Scholar's shortcomings, rattled off in numerous (and doubtfully read) FAQ lists, become a demonstrable part of the reference transaction, one important caveat at a time. The transactions with GS also offer information for planning a component for an instruction session, or for a specialized GS workshop geared toward faculty or students.

NOTES

1. E. Meltzer, "UC Libraries Use of Google Scholar" (August 2005). <http://www. cdlib.org/inside/assess/evaluation_activities/docs/2005/googleScholar_summary_0805. pdf>. (Accessed June 25, 2007, 1).

2. Rebecca Donlan and Rachel Cooke, "Running with the Devil: Accessing Library-Licensed Full Text Holdings Through Google Scholar," in *Libraries and Google*. Edited by William Miller and Rita Pellen. (Binghamton, NY: Haworth, 2005), 150.

3. Meltzer, 1.

4. Donlan and Cooke, 154.

5. Gail Golderman and Bruce Connolly. "Who Cited This?" *Library Journal*, January 15, 2007, 18.

6. Ed Tallent. "Metasearching in Boston College Libraries–A Case Study of User Reactions," *New Library World*, 105, no. 1196-1197 (2004): 71, 72.

7. Meltzer, 8.

8. Glenn Haya, Else Nygren, and Wilhelm Widmark, "Metalib and Google Scholar: A User Study," *Online Information Review*, 31, no. 3 (2007): 365-375.

9. Martin Kesselman and Sarah Barbara Watstein. "Google Scholar and Libraries: Point/Counterpoint," *Reference Services Review,* 33, no. 4 (2005): 386.

Google Book Search Libraries and Their Digital Copies

Jill E. Grogg
Beth Ashmore

Few things in the past decade, other than the PATRIOT Act, have brought libraries and subsequent controversy into the mainstream media as much as the Google Book Search Library Project.

For some–both inside and outside the profession–the mass digitization of library-owned books by Google sounded like yet another death knell for physical libraries and their custodial librarians alike. For others, it appeared to launch the mother of all copyright cases. However, in nearly every instance of media hype, the focus sat squarely on what Google planned to do with all those digitized books. While Google's intentions are always a good topic for conversation and as everyone waits for the courts to decide on important copyright issues, one can't help but wonder: How will the librarians at participating Google Book Search libraries use their copies of the digitized books, commonly referred to as the library digital copy, the copy that Google gave to them in return for their participation in the Book Search project?

Google Book Search participating libraries now include the University of California (UC), University Complutense of Madrid, Harvard University (Harvard), University of Michigan (UM), The New York Public Library (NYPL), Oxford University (Oxford), Stanford University (Stanford), University of Wisconsin-Madison (UW-Madison) and University of Virginia (UVA). In January 2007 alone, Google added two more library partners with the National Library of Catalonia merged with four affiliate Catalonian libraries and the University of Texas at Austin library. In February, Google added Princeton University's libraries and, in March, Bayerische Staatsbibliothek (Bavaria State Library). These libraries represent some of the largest and most impressive collections in existence anywhere in the world, and, in most cases, the deals that have been struck with Google are just as unique as the collections being housed. Some of the library administrators have chosen to focus on specific collections within their libraries, while others simply look for materials in good condition and in the public domain. Speaking of public domain, many library administrators have chosen to restrict themselves to these materials. Others either leave the door open to any materials within their collection, public domain or not, or purposefully choose to include in-copyright materials.

Once the contracts were signed, the scanning began at full speed. However, it is critical to note that while Google scanning has begun, partnering with Google is not the first experience these librarians have had with digital preservation and full-text searching of their digital content.

PRE-GOOGLE LIBRARY DIGITIZATION

The Google Book Search Library Project is extremely attractive because Google has the knowledge and the resources to shift a library's existing digitization program into high gear at the best possible budget allocation–nearly free. However, considering the immense and unique collections of the Google Book Search Library Project partners, it is no surprise that many of these libraries had thriving digitization projects underway long before Google came knocking.

University of Michigan, arguably the leader among the Google library partners, has been working on a variety of digitization initiatives since the late 1980s. Anne Karle-Zenith, special projects librarian, University Library, UM, cited the current statistics on their digitization progress prior to Google: "141 text collections with 25 million page images online, plus 3 million pages of encoded text and 89 image collections containing approximately 200,000 images." UM has also partnered with Cornell University to create the Making of America project, funded by the Mellon Foundation. Making of America has provided researchers with access to hundreds of volumes of American primary sources from 1850 to 1876. The established reputation of UM's library as a leader in digitization merely represents an outgrowth of its mission. Karle-Zenith explained: "Preservation and stewardship of our digital assets has always been one of our top priorities."

At New York Public Library, The Digital Gallery contains more than 520,000 images from the four research libraries: the Humanities and Social Sciences Library; The New York Public Library for the Performing Arts; the Schomburg Center for Research in Black Culture; and the Science, Industry and Business Library. David Ferriero, Andrew W. Mellon, director and chief executive of the NYPL Research Libraries, described The Digital Gallery as ". . . a kind of snapshot of collections from within the four research libraries." Another NYPL digitization project, "In Motion: The African American Migration Experience," comes from the Schomburg Center for Research in Black Culture with support from the Congressional Black Caucus and the Institute for Museum and Library Services. NYPL has other digitization efforts, all available under the moniker NYPL Digital, at <http://www.nypl.org/digital/index.htm>.

UW-Madison, a recent addition to the list of Google Library partners, is no stranger to digital preservation. Edward Van Gemert, interim director at the UW-Madison Libraries, explained: "We've collected, digitized, organized, and made available now close to 2 million pages of content with a full range of subjects and all of that material is available on our library Web site." UWMadison's current digitization projects, including its plans with Google, have a well-defined focus born directly out of the strength of its American history collections and its ongoing partnership with the Wisconsin Historical Society (WHS). By working with state and federal documents and other public domain materials that cover areas including "statehood, regional history, patents and discoveries," UW-Madison seeks to create a historical record of the formation of the United States, the upper Midwest, and the territory of Wisconsin. By playing to the strengths of its physical collections, UW-Madison seeks to establish a digital repository of primary resources in American history. The partnership among UW-Madison, WHS, and Google is designed to build upon this existing mission.

UM, NYPL, and UW-Madison are by no means alone in their pre-Google digitization endeavors. According to the University of California 2006 annual report <http://www.universityofcalifornia.edu/annual report/2006/pdf/fullreport_06.pdf>, "Calisphere, an online service of the UC Libraries and the California Digital Library, provides access to over 170,000 digital images and 50,000 pages of documents about California." The UC Libraries and the CDL have other digitization projects as well.

Dale Flecker, associate director of the Harvard University Library for Planning and Systems, noted, "Harvard has a strong and long-standing program in preserving digital information. We will use our digital preservation infrastructure to preserve the data created in our Google project." Michael Popham, head of the Oxford Digital Library, Oxford University Library Services, echoed Flecker's comments about long-standing programs: "We [Oxford] have undertaken a variety of digital preservation initiatives over many years across the university. For example, this year the Oxford Text Archive celebrated its 30th anniversary collecting, preserving, and freely disseminating electronic texts and corpora."

Finally, the University of Virginia is a long-time player in digital preservation. Karin Wittenborg, university librarian, UVA, noted, "We started, I think, the first electronic text center in the humanities back in 1992, and so we've been digitizing for a long, long time, and we know exactly how expensive it is." This digitization effort was originally called Etext but, according to Wittenborg, UVA has merged many texts and images into something it calls Scholars' Lab <http://www.lib.virginia. edu/scholarslab>. In the original Etext Center <http://etext.lib.virginia. edu/collections>, items scanned were all public domain materials.

At the end of the day, the participating libraries' existing projects represent an effort to achieve two key goals: to preserve materials for generations to come and to provide increased access and functionality for the generation at hand. With Google the favorite discovery tool among the current generation, it is easy to see how Google has become an important partner for libraries to further their digitization goals.

THE GOOGLE LIBRARY PARTY

Librarians participating in Google Book Search scanning can easily add links on their libraries' Web pages to the Google Book Search Web site <http://books.google.com> and call it a day. However, with the number of aforementioned in-house digitization projects, most librarians find great potential for using the copies they receive from Google in conjunction with existing library resources and newly created partnerships. And the future may see even nonmembers of the Google Library Party doing the same thing. As Megan Lamb, of Google Corporate Communications, explains "We've [Google] already done significant engineering work in ensuring that our URLs are persistent and any organization can link to them."

For example, Popham of Oxford explains the necessity for new partnerships to cope with the enormity of the Google project: "The sheer scale of our endeavor with Google vastly overshadows any previous [digitization] activity and will require additional preservation infrastructure, which we are developing in partnership with Sun Microsystems, as part of the establishment of a Sun Center of Excellence here in Oxford." While all of the participating Google Book Search libraries have digitization projects in existence, few, if any, approach the scale of the Google project. Jennifer Colvin, strategic communications manager, UC Office of the President, stated, "The university libraries have been doing other digitization projects for years, but nothing nearly on the scale of what we are doing with the OCA [Open Content Alliance] and with Google, so that's one of the reasons we are so excited about our partnerships with those organizations."

Such an increase in scale means that some library administrators are still weighing options about how to use their library digital copies. In August 2006, Barbara Quint reported in an Information Today, Inc., News-Break ("Google Book Search Adds Big, Brave Partner: The University of California") that "plans as to what UC intends to do with its digital copies are still in the works. However, public domain material will have free and unfettered full-text access throughout the system, including links to the online Melvyl Catalog. Books still in copyright will only be accessible in keeping with copyright law" <http://newsbreaks.info-today.com/nbReader.asp?ArticleId=17375>. According to Colvin, UC has organized a "system-wide group with representatives from across the UC system to try to figure out what the next step is going to be and how we can possibly integrate those digital books in with our collection." According to Flecker, Harvard is not using the data at this point: "Future uses are under discussion, but no concrete plans are in place." While no concrete plans may be in place, Harvard is enthusiastic about the possibilities the mass digitization offers. Flecker noted, "We are excited about the possibility of making the collection of scanned books available in the future for text mining, which we believe will open up powerful new ways of doing research."

NYPL's Ferriero envisions a future in which patrons conduct searches in its Digital Gallery and receive not only images from across the research libraries, but also the text that provides necessary context and avenues for further research. While NYPL is still making plans for how it will use its digital copies (in December, it just finished the Google pilot of 10,000 volumes and made arrangements to continue the relationship), it is carefully watching how other Google partners are putting their digital copies to work for them. In fact, the Google Library partners meet twice a year to take advantage of the lessons learned from each of their very individual ventures.

Like Harvard and the NYPL, Oxford continues to explore how best to use its digital copies. When asked to describe how his library currently uses and/or plans to use digital copies received from Google, Popham replied, "At the moment, we are simply planning to archive and preserve our copy of the data generated by our joint project with Google." Popham went on to say that Oxford will link from its catalog record to the images hosted at Google [http://books.google.com]. Finally, Popham explained, "The scale and scope of this project is such that we are only just beginning to consider some of the possibilities that this work may enable."

As one of the most recent of Google library partners, signing on in November 2006, UVA is understandably still considering how to use its digital copies. When asked if UVA was concentrating on specific subject areas, Wittenborg said, "We gave Google a lot of data on what we think our special strengths are, but they said essentially all 5.1 million volumes are still under consideration by them." Wittenborg went on to say, "They [Google and library partners] have a summit meeting of the [library] partners in January [2007] at Google, and so I think by then, if not before, we'll know. We are very, very strong in American literature and American history, but also in Buddhism and other things, so it's pretty much they get to choose." When asked if UVA was choosing to do both public domain and in-copyright materials, Wittenborg replied, "Absolutely. It was important for us to want to do the whole thing." Wittenborg emphasized the opportunity this presents for UVA: ". . . it's an open playing field. We know we'll be experimenting with software tools and delivery services, and our primary goal is to support research, teaching, and learning here at UVA. But I think that once we suddenly get content, we will find out there are all kinds of things we can do. I think there will be parts of the content that we will mark up for added value, but we just don't know yet."

UW-Madison, another new member of this exclusive club, has particular plans for organizing and providing access to the library's digital copies of Google-scanned material. Van Gemert stated: "Our intention is to have material searchable through our OPAC and our intention is to collaborate with other CIC [Committee on Institutional Cooperation] institutions on a shared digital repository." The CIC is a consortium of 12 major research universities, including those from the Big Ten athletic conference, along with the University of Chicago and the University of Illinois at Chicago. As mentioned earlier, UW-Madison also intends to leverage its investment in current digitization projects and, through its partnership with the Wisconsin Historical Society and Google, to create a larger, more comprehensive digital collection. Van Gemert explained, "Our primary focus is to have digitized materials in the public domain–state and federal government documents, other historical documents." While UW-Madison has a clear focus, it has yet to begin scanning; the operational side of its project with Google will begin in March 2007.

In addition to UW-Madison, the CIC group also includes UM, which, to date, has one of the most developed systems for providing access to its Google scanned materials–MBooks. MBooks allows patrons to discover books through full-text searching in its online catalog, Mirlyn. Once a title is identified, a patron can click on a link, which takes them to a "page turner" interface that allows them to navigate the book, print individual pages, and enlarge and rotate the page image as well as to search within that individual title. The library digital copies delivered to UM are individual pages–mostly 600 dpi TIFF images using ITU G4 compression, although pages with significant illustrations usually appear as 300 dpi JPEG 2000 images. Google also provides an OCR text file to match each page image. The type of image files provided to a library depends on the library's preferences <http://www.lib.umich.edu/staff/google/public/faq.pdf>. While one cannot print out entire PDF files of a single title from the MBooks interface, the MBooks record does provide links back to the Google Book Search copy.

Because UM is one of the libraries allowing Google to scan in-copyright titles, MBooks provides searching within these titles, as well as information on the number of occurrences and location of terms within an individual title, to assist the user in evaluating the relevance of the item to their research. MBooks currently only houses the titles scanned through Google, but there are plans to add materials from previous in-house digitization efforts to the database as well.

PUBLIC REACTION

The media has definitely taken a shine to the Google Book Search Library Project. However, Google is not the first to try to take the world of public domain online. Initiatives such as the Internet Archive, Project Gutenberg, and American Memory have all tread much of the same ground as Google. So, why all the fuss? Some of the attention can be traced back to Google's high recognition factor, which inevitably makes its new endeavors newsworthy. And then Google is clearly navigating some uncharted waters for fair use. The speed and scope of the effort, covering such a large amount of materials in a relatively short amount of time, also draws attention.

Karle-Zenith summed it up: "This is a very ambitious project that will provide scholars and the general public with an unprecedented ability to search for and locate books from the university's vast collections. This initiative has the potential to revolutionize the way the world's knowledge is transmitted and to democratize access to information. However, throughout history, breakthroughs in technology have always created challenges." Wittenborg also commented about the media fascination with Google: "I think the media is captivated because Google is changing the game. The rest of us were moving very slowly with public domain . . . and suddenly everything is different. The potential for discovery at this level of magnitude of millions of titles is going to be incredible."

While the media may be taking notice, users still seem to be a bit confused over what exactly this project means for their own research. "I think there is a fair amount of concern over what this all means for the future," Ferriero explained, adding that he thinks there is a great deal of excitement about the ability to search full text. "The fact that the New York Public Library has decided to include public domain material only is different from some of the other partners, and I think that's not clear in some people's minds, so they expect to see content that hasn't been digitized."

If the differences between the arrangements that Google has made with each of its library partners have led to confusion on the part of users, it has not prevented new library partners from seeing the advantages to signing up. "Campus administration was clearly supportive and clearly excited about the project," Van Gemert said of UW-Madison's recent negotiations with Google. "We see it, of course, as a way to get a huge amount of material digitized for a relatively low cost."

The library administrators were nearly unanimous in responding that their respective constituencies were supportive of the project. Popham of Oxford noted, "On the whole, the reaction had been extremely positive." However, similar to Ferriero's comments about general confusion, Popham said, "Most of the reservations that have been expressed to us have been based on a misunderstanding of the nature of the project, or the way the digitized materials will be made available. For example, the most common misconceptions are that access to the digital copies of materials from our collections will be restricted to users at Oxford, or that people will have to pay to access the digital materials; in fact, neither is the case." Therefore, while the media has showered much attention on certain aspects of the Google Book Search Project, it will still be incumbent on librarians at participating libraries to educate their users about the realities of participation.

COPYRIGHT AND OTHER CONCERNS

In any discussion of Google Book Search, the 800-pound gorilla in the room is copyright, or, more accurately, litigation over copyright. In the fall of 2005, both the Association of American Publishers (AAP) and the Authors' Guild filed suits against Google over Google's library scanning project. Jim Milliot summed up the major issues behind the AAP's suit in an October 24, 2006, column in *Publisher's Weekly*: "The lawsuit reflects a deep division between publishers and Google over the meaning of fair use. Google compares scanning books to its copying of materials online, a comparison the publishers contend is faulty." The fact that there is so much ambiguity over what constitutes fair use will come as no surprise to information professionals, but the serious way in which a critical mass of the publishing community has banded together on this issue is noteworthy. "Google has positioned its library project as part of its mission to make all the world's information available," Milliot explains, "but publishers see scanning of copyrighted materials without permission as the first step in the loss of control over their content."

It appears that for copyright holders, the stakes could not be higher, making the likelihood of publishers backing down fairly low. No doubt, the library administrators involved in the scanning of in-copyright material have taken this copyright smackdown into consideration before signing on with Google. As a matter of fact, one library declined comment for this article partly due to the pending litigation. When asked to be interviewed, Michael A. Keller, university librarian; director of academic information resources; publisher of HighWirePress; and publisher of Stanford University Press, Stanford University, noted that Stanford preferred to comment about its intentions for its digital copies "only after we have actually accomplished some of the programs and functions that we anticipate implementing." Keller further explained, "It would be a mistake for anyone at Stanford involved in the project to respond to some of your questions before the suits against Google in the Southern District of the Second Circuit of the U.S. courts have been heard and decisions made and publicized." Should readers be interested in Stanford's participation, Keller pointed to a number of Web sites, such as <http://library.stanford.edu/about_sulair/news_and_events/stanford_google_project.html>.

With both Google and publishers seemingly equally convinced of their legal footing in the ensuing battle over fair use, most library administrators appear to be taking a safe approach to scanning. For many years, librarians have been trying to discern the best way to comply with copyright while providing as much access as possible. It is not easy for librarians to let go of years of cautious interpretation of fair use, but some are making an effort. UM's Karle-Zenith stated, "We believe Google is making a lawful copy." However, she also noted, "The library is assuming little to no risk because, per our contract, Google indemnifies us against any third-party claim that the project violates third-party's copyrights or other legal rights."

Even with UM's relatively safe approach to in-copyright scanning, many library partners are still going the public domain route–for more than simple legal reasons. "We wouldn't get involved until there's a decision on the two lawsuits," NYPL's Ferriero explained. "The rationale is that we're here in New York City in the middle of the corporate publishing empire, and many of those publishers' names are carved in gold on our walls. So, we are nervous about getting into that arena." In addition to trying to keep up amicable relations with publishers, some library administrators see public domain as a big enough task already. "There's a huge amount of material in the public domain . . . there's a whole category of material that falls into that orphan class of material that is indistinguishable . . . so that is an area where we will probably move into next," UWMadison's Van Gemert explained. With a world of pre-1923 titles waiting for attention and legal decisions yet to be decided, the hassle of in-copyright scanning would appear to be too much for most participating libraries to attempt–at least for now.

Partnering with Google on any project carries with it some concerns of its own. Brewster Kahle, founder of the Open Content Alliance (OCA), has expressed concerns that Google is building "the private library" of a single corporation rather than a public resource, and questions whether or not this is the right kind of project for libraries to become involved in (*Library Journal*, Oct. 1, 2006). Many library partners see this not so much as an opportunity to help Google build its own library, but instead a situation where both parties reach their goals through collaboration. "The University [of Michigan] has a long history of collaborating with private corporations when we can find areas of common interest and can work together to produce fruitful outcomes on both sides," explained Karle-Zenith. Other library partners seem to take a different tack, participating in many digitization efforts at once. For example, UC is a member of the OCA, Google Book Search, and Microsoft Live Search Books, as well as other digitization initiatives. When asked about UC's decision to participate in multiple initiatives, Colvin replied, "I think this goes back to our mission as a public university and our goal to make as much information available as possible. We are happy to work with anyone who will help us achieve those goals." Like UC, UVA is also a member of the OCA.

Still other librarians feel it is necessary to take steps to ensure that Google's program is in line with their library's mission. As Van Gemert explained, "Anytime you go into a large project like this that represents significant change . . . there's going to be concern. Some folks definitely want to talk about what safeguards we've put in place to obey copyright, to maintain a research library in terms of collection, whether they be print or electronic, and proper preservation activities . . ."

The concerns don't end there. With so many partners sticking to their public domain collections, there is some question of the value of these materials to the average user. In his February 5, 2005, *Library Journal* column, Roy Tennant questions whether or not we are doing users any favors by adding a plethora of pre-1923 information to the already authority-shaky Internet: "Unfortunately, I can think of few situations where having access to only pre-1923 literature is a good thing. The typical user who finds a pre-1923 source available for free via Google is unlikely to sashay down to the local library for something more recent. That's just life." While many information professionals would echo Tennant's sentiments, Karle-Zenith sees this as no reason to dump the project: "How could access to only pre-1923 literature be better than access to no literature? We have seen the value of pre-1923 content time and again, with, for example, the Making of America [MoA] project. . . . The response from scholars has been enthusiastic from the time the MoA materials first went online. . . . To this day we continue to hear from users about new discoveries and new knowledge generated by their research on Making of America." Like the enthusiastic scholar reaction to MoA, UVA's Wittenborg commented on the "extraordinary number of downloads" from UVa's Etext Center, which contains, in addition to other items, a number of digital copies of 18th- and 19th-century books. "Suddenly," Wittenborg said, "these books found an audience."

Furthermore, some librarians and university administrators have expressed that partnering with Google is simply "the right thing to do." Wyatt R. Hume, UC executive vice president and provost, expressed precisely this sentiment in an August 9, 2006, press release <http://www.universityofcalifornia.edu/news/2006/aug09.html>. In the same press release, Brian E. C. Schottlander, university librarian at UC San Diego, rationalized that participation with Google is a solution to urgent problems of preservation, giving Hurricane Katrina as a prime example of the type of natural disaster that can wreak havoc.

Whatever the reason for participation, whatever the rationale and accompanying concerns, the simple fact remains that Google can offer digitization on a grand scale at a price libraries can afford. When asked if Harvard was participating in any other large digitization initiatives (e.g., American Memory, Project Gutenberg, Million Book Project, OCA, Universal Library), Flecker explained, "No, we are not participating in any of these other projects at this point. Google approached Harvard with a proposal to do large-scale digitization at their expense. No one else has such made such a proposal." However, Flecker qualified, "Our agreement with Google is non-exclusive, and we would be very open to working with other digitization initiatives. Increasing the corpus of digitized materials available across the Internet is a major priority of the Harvard libraries."

Flecker's comments point to an important issue within the Google Book Search Library Project: exclusivity, or the lack thereof. As mentioned earlier, Kahle of the OCA has concerns over Google's motives to build "a private library," but in conversations with administrators at the participating libraries, non-exclusivity was a common theme. For example, when asked how digitization partnerships with current for-profit vendors such as ProQuest would be affected, NYPL's Ferriero responded unequivocally, "All agreements we sign are non-exclusive, meaning it is possible that multiple vendors could film or scan the same text." Librarians are not in the business of limiting access but rather increasing it, so partnering with Google may seem like a logical next step in any digitization program.

Moreover, partnering with Google is not the only option. In addition to digitization initiatives, such as those elsewhere in this article (i.e., American Memory, Project Gutenberg, Million Book Project, Open Content Alliance, Universal Library, Making of America), Microsoft has its own rival book-scanning project. In the December 17, 2006, Chronicle of Higher Education The Wired Campus column, Microsoft's Live Search Books is discussed: "It may seem like Google's much-debated book-scanning project has secured the participation of every library under the sun. But Microsoft's less-discussed rival project has managed to recruit some pretty big names of its own–including the British Library, the University of California, and the University of Toronto" <http://chronicle.com/wiredcampus/article/1759/microsoft-releases-rival-to-googlesbook-scanning-project>. Again we see the results of librarians' commitment to non-exclusivity, which translates into a commitment to access: getting the right book to the right reader at the right time.

The public at large may be encouraged by discussions such as those within the CIC to build common digital repositories, and with not one but two participating Google Book Search libraries, the prospects look good. The simple fact that libraries are receiving their own digital copies goes a long way to allay fears of "the private library." Karle-Zenith of UM emphasized, "We are receiving our own copies of the digitized volumes so we can ensure they are preserved for future generations and made accessible as a public resource. While this may not be Google's mission, it is the mission of the library and we take this very seriously." Indeed, most libraries and librarians alike take the notion of unfettered access to library materials very seriously, hence the long-standing differences of opinions between librarians and publishers.

In terms of other concerns relating to participation in the Google project, all of the librarians interviewed were asked about any restrictions Google placed on their use of the digital copies (other than copyright restrictions). While the specific restrictions contained in some of the agreements are under nondisclosure, Popham of Oxford said, "We do not consider them onerous, nor an impediment to the scholarly uses to which we envisage the data might be put." Furthermore, when asked about any initial concerns relating to participation in the Google project, Popham said, "We only had two major concerns about participating in the project. First, that the digitization process should not result in any more damage to the physical condition of the materials chosen, other than what we might expect to see if a reader were to consult one of the books in our reading rooms. Second, that we would not be unduly constrained in our ability to reuse the resulting digital data for scholarly purposes."

Karle-Zenith of UM echoes Popham's comments about initial participation reservations: "We wanted to ensure that we would receive images that adhere to library preservation standards, and we do. . . . We wanted a guarantee that our materials would not be damaged or destroyed in the process of digitization. . . . We were concerned about having the appropriate rights to utilize our copy in ways that are consistent with the library's mission." Karle-Zenith was also able to discuss some specific restrictions: UM is required to restrict automated access to its digital copy and to take measures to prevent third parties from either downloading its copy for commercial purposes or redistributing any portions of its copy. UM must also restrict automated and systematic downloading of the image files from its copy. Indeed, at least in UM's case, these specific restrictions do not appear overly onerous, as Popham put it. We are nowhere near to hearing the last word on how participating libraries will use the digital copies received through the Google Book Search Library Project. With more libraries climbing aboard the project on a regular basis, the possibilities are both complicated and endless. Perhaps Popham said it best: "What Google brought was an exciting vision and the resources to make that a reality."

1923–THE CUT-OFF POINT

Public domain status is a critical issue in the Google Book Library project. When does it start? Where does it apply? The issue became even more critical when Google changed its original policy and began providing PDF downloads of entire public domain titles–at least to U.S. users. From what we can gather the libraries that only open public domain content to Google digitization determine whether something is public domain or not. In practice, however, the issue seems to devolve to whether an item was published before 1923. In other words, because there is so much pre-1923 content and because it takes so much effort to determine whether something post-1923 is public domain or not (life of the author plus 80 years of his dog's life, or whatever), the public domain-only libraries seem to focus on only pre-1923 material at this point.

COPYRIGHT, SCHMOPYRIGHT

Who's Scanning What?

Much, if not all, of the controversy surrounding the Google Book Search Library Project stems from the scanning of in-copyright material. But how many of the library partners have actually chosen to make their entire collections possible candidates for scanning? Once the courts decide where Google stands in regard to copyright, these partners may switch sides, but for now, here's how they line up.

Libraries sticking with public domain (at least for now):

- University Complutense of Madrid
- Harvard University
- The New York Public Library
- Oxford University
- Princeton University
- University of Wisconsin-Madison National
- Library of Catalonia and affiliates

Libraries open to scanning materials regardless of copyright status (at least until the courts decide):

- University of California
- University of Michigan
- Stanford University
- University of Texas
- University of Virginia

HOLE IN THE OZONE: THAT'S NEXT

In the March 2007 *Searcher*, Barbara Quint's editorial ("To the Ozone and Beyond") advocated that OCLC take a leadership role in expanding the impact of Google Book Search Library Project. In the course of researching this article, we came upon a scoop! Talk about quick service!

There are still a lot of unanswered questions when it comes to the on-going maintenance and development of the library sides of the project. As Karle-Zenith of the University of Michigan explained, "[Library] partners discuss mechanisms for creating links to the materials, whether held locally or at Google, how to represent the content in OCLC, strategies for storage, and how to account for and represent copyright in the digitized material."

Some of these answers may come from outside Google and the participating libraries, for example, from sources such as OCLC. Robert J. Murphy, senior public relations specialist at OCLC, explains how OCLC plans to assist librarians in increasing the access to the digital library copy beyond their local community. "We're planning a pilot program beginning in June to link to digitized book titles from WorldCat," said Murphy. "We are working with libraries contributing content to these mass digitization efforts to enable links from WorldCat. We will focus on books to start, adding other formats, such as serials, in later phases." As this pilot project by OCLC demonstrates, librarians and library stakeholders have a deep-rooted tradition of collaboration and information-sharing. As these and other unanswered questions arise, all parties will no doubt work to answer them together, drawing on a wealth of common experience from the participating libraries.

To Google or Not to Google, That Is the Question: Supplementing Google Book Search to Make It More Useful for Scholarship

Shawn Martin

INTRODUCTION

A recent review of the Google Book Search project by Robert Townsend, the Assistant Director of Research and Publications at the American Historical Association, states that

> The Google Books [sic] project promises to open up a vast amount of older literature, but a closer look at the material on the site raises

real worries about how well it can fulfill that promise and what its real objectives might be . . . from a researcher's point of view I have to say the results were deeply disconcerting.[1]

This assessment is only partially fair since Google is still working on the project and may very well improve some of the problems Townsend addresses. Nevertheless he is correct in one respect. Google does not (and may never) fully meet the needs of scholars. Why? By looking at just one aspect of the Google project, primarily its capabilities for full-text searching (or searching words within the book) it is possible to see Google's weaknesses. It is important though not to see these weaknesses as insurmountable, but to recognize when Google will likely be helpful and when it will not. When Google is not helpful, it is important to realize that it is possible to change that. Projects like the Text Creation Partnership (TCP) which aims to enhance commercial products similar to Google in many respects, is just one possible way to accomplish that. To badly paraphrase Shakespeare, it is not a question of whether "to Google or Not to Google." Instead it is a question of when it is appropriate to use the Google product for text searching, when to use other products for searching, and when to enhance Google to make it usable.

THE TEXT CREATION PARTNERSHIP

Before going too far though, it might be helpful to explain a bit about what the Text Creation Partnership (TCP) is. The project takes images from commercially published databases, in particular Early English Books Online (EEBO) published by ProQuest Information and Learning, Evans Early American Imprints from Newsbank-Readex, and Eighteenth Century Collections Online (ECCO) from Thomson-Gale. These three databases photographed pages of nearly every book printed in England and America between 1479 and 1800 (around three hundred thousand titles) into microfilm reels which they later converted to digital images.

In the Evans and ECCO collections, optical character recognition or OCR was used in the same way that Google has used it. The problem with OCR however is twofold. First the accuracy of OCR is not great. So it often transcribes words incorrectly, especially when there are odd fonts. Second, OCR does not recognize the structure of the text. There is no differentiation for paragraphs, typeface changes, italics, or the like. In the case of EEBO, most of the collection was in early modern Gothic fonts which are very difficult to read and scan accurately. Therefore, using OCR on that collection would have been useless.

The only way to remedy this problem completely would be to have human beings hand type the text, an incredibly expensive proposition. Also, to make the texts useful for scholarship, they have to have machine readable structure so that paragraphs, chapters, changes in typeface, or other textual features can be identified. OCR cannot do this; only a person manually inserting that information can. TCP was created so that all of this could be accomplished in a cost effective manner and benefit both publishers and the scholars and librarians who ultimately use these electronic collections.

How does TCP do this? Instead of relying on a computer to read the book and extract readable text from an image (as OCR does), TCP works with companies whose employees read the text, transcribe it, and add structural tagging (that allows a computer to see elements of the book such as paragraphs, typeface changes, and chapters). Normally two people type out and tag the text simultaneously and then a third person reviews both texts to see if there are any discrepancies which he or she then corrects. Finally staff at Michigan and Oxford, most of whom have advanced degrees in the humanities and experience in electronic editing, then review the books to see if there are any additional errors. If the book is less than 99.995% accurate (or there is more than one error per twenty thousand letters), the book is rejected and has to be redone. In other words TCP makes all of the texts it creates as accurate as possible given the constraints of a small staff and difficult materials.

The Universities of Michigan and Oxford, along with hundreds of other universities around the world, first attempted this with titles in EEBO and later expanded to the Evans and ECCO collections. TCP has now transcribed over fifteen thousand texts with a goal of completing forty thousand texts at the end of the project (approximately twenty percent of the total from the three collections). Moreover, TCP created an agreement with all three publishers that every text that the TCP created would eventually enter the public domain within five years after the completion of the project. So, eventually the transcribed texts of all of these books, the images of which are currently locked up behind publisher walls, will be open to the world both inside and outside of the academy.[2]

As a result of TCP's accuracy and more open intellectual property policies, scholars at over two hundred TCP member universities around the world are using the content for a wide variety of purposes. Some are searching for particular people or places. Others are looking for easily readable teaching editions (having students read the modern font TCP editions rather than the Gothic font original editions). Still others find it useful for compiling concordances or word lists for other kinds of research.[3]

WHAT DOES TCP HAVE TO DO WITH GOOGLE?

Technically nothing (at least not yet), but the problems of full-text searching in Google are similar to those faced in EEBO, Evans, and ECCO. Similarly, EEBO, Evans, and ECCO were initially created as commercial products focusing primarily on scanning books, like the cooperative digitization project between the University of Michigan and Google. When Google approached the University of Michigan to digitize its collection of seven million books along with those of several other libraries, it was a natural extension of Google's mission "to organize the world's information and make it universally accessible and useful." From Google's point of view having millions of works in its search engine and integrating those books with already existing products like Google Scholar helped to make the product more useful, attract more people to its site, and in the long term probably increase profits.

From the University of Michigan's point of view Google could digitize the library collection in only seven years at no cost or library staff could do the same thing in around one thousand years at tremendous cost. Additionally, the University of Michigan Library could offer up these books in the same way it has done with projects like the Making of America <http://www.hti.umich.edu/m/moagrp/> and other digitization projects.[4]

In the same way that EEBO, Evans, and ECCO faced complaints from the academic community about their lack of accurate full-text searching, Google will no doubt face the same problems. Currently, Google does an admirable job of making content available to the general reader; it does not presently serve all of the needs of scholarly audiences.

WHAT GOOGLE CANNOT DO FOR SCHOLARS (YET)

Unlike general readers, academic researchers need to do different things with electronic collections. They are interested in more than just the content of a book. Historians may be interested in contextualizing books in terms of larger events and trends in particular periods of time. Literary scholars might be interested in tracking typographical variants, changes in the structure of the book, and the syntactic elements of particular sentences. Linguists might be interested in finding the frequency of particular words in different eras. It is also important for all scholars to gather references, to see where particular people or places are mentioned and how often, to see what other books are being cited and why, and to see how concepts and ideas change over time. Therefore, though it is theoretically possible to do this kind of research with digital images and OCR text, to do that kind of work would require reading every word in over three hundred thousand books, an impossible feat. Google is currently not designed to enable this kind of in-depth research.

Two examples that highlight this problem can be found in Google's own books. At the University of Michigan's homepage for the Michigan Digitization Project (the official name for the cooperative scanning project with Google Book Search) to be found at <http://www.lib.umich. edu/mdp/>, the first book listed is *Football for player and spectator* by Fielding Yost (Ann Arbor, 1905).[5] Image fifteen is the beginning of a section entitled "Football: Its Origin and Development." If one switches from the page image view to the text view (which shows the OCR text used to search the book), one sees that rather than the title reading as it is printed, it is instead "Football: Its orioin and development." This is a common problem with OCR software, reading strange fonts (like the heading on this particular page).

A more egregious example can be found in the second book listed on the Michigan Digitization Project page, *The songs and music of Friedrich Froebel's Mother play (Mutter und kose lieder)* by Friedrich Froebel (New York, 1898).[6] Image twenty-six displays a German Poem printed in Fraktur script (similar in some ways to the Gothic scripts found in EEBO) which is clearly legible to anyone who is used to reading nineteenth century German printing. Yet again, if one looks at the full text for this page, it looks nothing like what is printed on the page. If one is simply paging through the book and reading it, this is not a problem. If, however, one is attempting to do linguistic searching on particular words and needs to find every instance of a word within the Google corpus, it is impossible to with the currently existing tools.

These kinds of problems are exactly what TCP was designed to remedy. With a human being physically typing in text and adding structural tagging, it is possible not only for scholars to be sure that they find every instance of a particular word, but that they can also perform advanced searches currently impossible in Google Book Search. Examples of this might include proximity searches (searching for a particular word next to another one, phrase searches (looking for a particular phrase as it appears exactly in the text), searches in particular parts of the text (like introductions, summaries, quotations, or the like). Advanced searching is essential for academic researchers who are asking very specific questions of the text. OCR text, like that which Google provides, allows researchers only to ask very general questions and may retrieve some but not all works relevant to particular questions. Structured text like TCP provides the ability to find every word with accuracy that is necessary for academic audiences.

ENHANCING GOOGLE THE TCP WAY

At its core, the TCP project is about several things: adding value to existing collections, creating a core canon of electronic materials all adhering to the same standard, providing a foundation of electronic materials for other projects to use, and creating an infrastructure by which to do all of this. EEBO, Evans, and ECCO made almost every book printed in English between 1470 and 1800 available electronically. Google will make a significant portion of books created between 1800 and the present available. As with EEBO, Evans, and ECCO, the digitization of books in Google is a major step forward, but it was not sufficient to meet all of the needs of scholars, particularly those who wish to use electronic media to their fullest.[7] TCP can provide the next step.

The need to enhance OCR text for collections like Google is very apparent. It is also important from an academic library perspective to think about building an electronic collection that will meet future library needs, to create a canon of material to a common standard. This is particularly important for library preservation and for teaching. Authors like Shakespeare, Swift, and Wheatley are seminal to studying English and American Literature; Acts of Parliament and royal proclamations, religious sermons, and miscellaneous pamphlets are essential in understanding early modern culture. From a library standpoint, it is likely that teachers and students will need to use this material many years from now. So it makes sense to create standard editions of it which are no longer locked up by copyright law and are available for classroom or research use. It also makes sense for the library to preserve standardized editions of these authors and books in the same way that it has preserved the print editions of these works.

TCP has also stimulated the development of nearly twenty other projects to date. Most notable is a tool created by scholars at Northwestern University that standardizes early modern spelling variants (in early English books, it is not uncommon to see words like "saint" spelled sainte, saynt, or even sayncte). The library at the University of Chicago has loaded EEBO-TCP texts into PhiloLogic, a database used primarily by linguists. TCP is also working with an electronic Spenser collection based at Washington University–St. Louis, a project on early modern witchcraft at the University of Alberta, and even a cyberinfrastructure project at the University of Victoria.[8] All of these projects have used TCP as the foundation of the scholarly edition, database, tool, or research project.

In many cases, projects might have been impossible without resources like TCP. The cost of creating thousands of electronic works is expensive, and why should twenty individual projects basically pay to do the same work over and over again, when one project can do the same work once and then distribute it? So, TCP can reduce the costs and make smaller scholarly projects possible. Google has the same kind of potential. Think what scholars of nineteenth century America could do with an accurate and searchable collection of the thousands of books Google will be digitizing from that period. Think of what will be possible with secondary works (works analyzing these nineteenth-century books) for future scholars once they enter the public domain. Google can and probably will become a center of scholarly activity for the nineteenth century in the same way TCP has already become one for the sixteenth century.

This leads to one last point. TCP is not just a way of enhancing collections of digital images. It is also a model for librarians, faculty, publishers, and other groups interested in the electronic publishing and scholarly communication communities to come together for a common cause. TCP is supported by over two hundred different libraries and three publishers contributing parts of their budgets to help create these texts. So far Google is supported only by a handful of libraries, but it is a project that is constantly growing. The more money TCP brings in, the more texts the project can create, and, therefore, each text becomes less expensive as the collection expands. Few academic projects have managed to create thousands of e-texts in only five years as TCP has done, and it has only done so because of the support of publishers. With the support of Google, libraries coming together for another common cause (enhancing the Google Book Search collection) could have an even greater impact. This kind of model would be a more sustainable way of creating large collections than grants or other traditional methods of digital library creation. Up to now, the TCP model has only been used for three very particular collections, but could easily be expanded to include not only a canon of important books within the Google collection but also journal articles, databases of scientific materials, and institutional repositories.

Nor would the TCP model necessarily be limited to e-texts. Similar groups could come together to enhance metadata, fill in gaps within the Google collection (if there are particular kinds of books that are not being scanned), improve scanning quality in books, or build tools to better search the materials within Google and other collections. According to the final report of the American Council of Learned Societies (ACLS) Committee on Cyberinfrastructure "Certainly the definition and construction of the cyberinfrastructure should be a collaborative, shared undertaking involving the humanities and social sciences community in the broadest sense." The report also states that

> Much of the recent leadership within the academy on issues of digitization in the humanities and social sciences has not come directly from scholars, but from librarians. As the library constitutes the historic infrastructure of scholarship, it is entirely appropriate that librarians have sought to re-ignite scholarly engagement with infrastructural issues.[9]

TCP is certainly not the only way to create such a shared cyber-infrastructure, but it is a successful model that may help us to think about the next steps once Google and other mass digitization projects are completed.

CONCLUSIONS

It is important that the academic community realize three things. First, Google Book Search allows for general searching with OCR that does not support academic research. Projects like TCP offer an enhanced searching that is better for investigating particular scholarly questions. Second, the academic community does not necessarily have to look to Google in order to make the Google Book Search collection more useful for scholarly research. Third, there are ways that libraries, Google, and other groups can help to improve the resource.

TCP has successfully enhanced collections by commercial publishers for many years now. It is possible for scholars, librarians, and publishers to come together in similar ways to think about what the Google project offers now, and what it could offer in the future. Linguists may want to extract word lists; literary scholars may want to create editions of particular authors; historians may want to create do full-text searching on specific people or events. Some of these functions may have commercial value for Google to pursue. Other operations may only be valuable to a narrow audience and will need to be developed by universities. So instead of looking at Google Book Search as it stands now and assuming that it is either unusable or that Google will fix everything, rather the academic community should think about ways to improve the collection much as what the TCP has already done with EEBO, Evans, and ECCO. The Google project lends itself to value added projects like TCP, and now is the time to strategize how to add value to this important collection. In other words it is not a question of whether to Google or not to Google; it is a question of when to Google and when to enhance Google.

NOTES

1. Review "Google Books: What's not to Like" (April 30, 2007), <http://blog. historians.org/articles/204/google-books-whats-not-to-like>. (Accessed August 17, 2007).

2. More information about the TCP project is available at <http:// www.lib.umich. edu/tcp>. (Accessed August 17, 2007). There are also several articles written about it including several by Mark Sandler, the founder of the project. See Mark Sandler, "New Uses for the World's Oldest Books: Democratizing Access to Historic Corpora," *ARL Bimonthly Report*, 232 (February 2004): 4-6. Mark Sandler, "The Early English Books Online C Text Creation Partnership," *The Charleston Advisor*, 4, no. 4 (April 2003): 47-49.

3. For a more complete overview of the different kinds of research that people are doing with TCP collections, see Shawn Martin, "Collaboration in Electronic Scholarly Communication: New Possibilities for Old Books" *Journal of the Association for History and Computing*, IX, No. 2 (October, 2006), <http://mcel.pacificu.edu/jahc/ jahcix2/articles/martin.htm>. (Accessed August 17, 2007).

4. The University of Michigan Library has actually already begun work on an interface for its books digitized by Google. More information about this is available at <http://www.lib.umich.edu/mdp/>.

5. Available at <http://mdp.lib.umich.edu/cgi/pt?id=39015002370743>. (Accessed August 17, 2007).

6. Available at <http://mdp.lib.umich.edu/cgi/pt?id=39015062755353>. (Accessed August 17, 2007).

7. For more information about the differences between traditional and electronic scholarship, and the needs to move the digital humanities forward, see Shawn Martin, "Digital Scholarship and Cyberinfrastructure in the Humanities: Lessons from the Text Creation Partnership," *Journal of Electronic Publishing*, 10, No. 1 (January, 2007), <http://hdl.handle.net/2027/spo.3336451.0010.105>. (Accessed August 17, 2007).

8. More specific information about these projects is also available in Shawn Martin, "Digital Scholarship and Cyberinfrastructure in the Humanities: Lessons from the

Text Creation Partnership," *Journal of Electronic Publishing*, 10, No. 1 (January, 2007), <http://hdl.handle.net/2027/spo.3336451.0010.105>. (Accessed August 17, 2007).

9. John Unsworth et al. "Our Cultural Commonwealth: The final report of the American Council of Learned Societies Commission on Cyberinfrastructure for the Humanities & Social Sciences," (December 13, 2006) pp. 48-49 <http://www.acls.org/cyberinfrastructure/acls.ci.report.pdf>. (Accessed August 17, 2007).

The Million Book Project
in Relation to Google

Gloriana St. Clair

VISION AND LINEAGE

The vision of Google Book Search and its predecessors, the Million Book Project (a program of the Universal Library), and Project Gutenberg, is to bring all scholarly content to the web so that it can be easily searched and read by students, scholars, and citizens worldwide. The achievement of this vision would benefit society and the scholarly enterprise.

Google Book Search, previously named Google Print, has garnered the highest name recognition among projects attempting to bring monographic content to the web. Google's wealth has allowed it to make a big splash with its initial announcement, especially because of its ongoing battles with publishers over copyright, and with its steady additions to its list of partner libraries.

Google Book Search is now the most well-known book digitization project, but it is by no means the only one. Its "News and Views" page lists several projects that inspired it, and this discussion primarily covers those projects and a successor project, the Open Content Alliance. Several other countries also have even larger digital collections, such as China's Superstore, Japan's National Diet Library, and an extensive collection in Korea.

Table 1 below attempts to quantify the projects that Google acknowledges.[1] The Library of Congress's American Memory project has nine million items. This early and ambitious project includes historical documents, photographs, sound recordings, moving pictures, books, pamphlets and maps. For rough measurement purposes, twenty items were deemed to equal a book, so one could say that the project includes 450,000 books. Project Gutenberg, another early attempt that involved keying in texts, claims to have over 17,000 books in its collection.

The Million Book Project

Funded by the National Science Foundation (NSF) beginning in 2000, the Million Book Project, under the direction of Carnegie Mellon

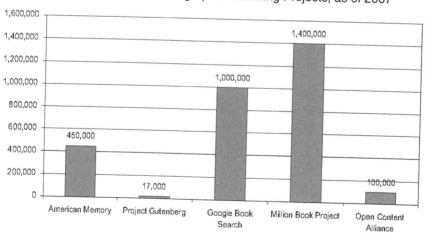

TABLE 1. Large U.S. Monographic Scanning Projects, as of 2007

computer scientists–Dr. Raj Reddy, Dr. Jaime Carbonell, Dr. Michael Shamos and Dean of Libraries Dr. Gloriana St. Clair, is a cooperative international project with universities in China and India, the Biblioteca Alexandrina, and a variety of other partners. The over 1.4 million books scanned in the project are accessible at web sites in India and China: <http://www.ernet.dli.in> and <http://www.ulib.org.cn>. NSF funding supported the purchase of equipment and some travel and labor; other project costs were supported by funding from the governments of China and India. Most material in the project comes from libraries in China, India, and Egypt, and is in the many languages used in those countries.

The National Science Foundation funded the project in order to set off a paradigm change in the approach toward monograph scanning. When the Google Book Search project began, NSF program officers acknowledged that their hopes in funding the Million Book Project had been realized. The Million Book Project used these rationales with NSF:

- Tremendous disparity exists across the nation and around the world in the size and accessibility of library collections. Some single institutions, like Harvard and Yale, have more books in their libraries than some entire states have in all their libraries combined.
- In our rapidly changing world, lifelong learning and access to books have become essential to employment health, peace, and prosperity. Greater public access to information is consistent with the goals of education and democracy.
- The expectation is that greater access to information will enhance respect for diversity and pluralism, alter the ways in which people work and deliberate together, and better equip people to understand and challenge the world around them.
- Equitable, worldwide access to the Million Book collection will contribute to the democratization of knowledge and empowerment of a global citizenry.
- A very important aspect of the Million Book Project is that it creates a huge digital test bed that stimulates and supports research in information storage and management, search engines, image processing, and machine translation.

A primary purpose of the Million Book Project is to create a test bed for advancing research and development in computer science and related areas, including

- Machine translation
- Massive distributed databases
- Storage formats
- Use of digital libraries
- Distribution and sustainability
- Security
- Search engines
- Image processing
- Optical character recognition
- Language processing
- Copyright law

Researchers from the partner countries meet annually to exchange views and best practices at an International Conference on the Universal Digital Library (ICUDL).[2]

In 2003, project participants met with the President of India Dr. A. P. J. Abdul Kalam. In his book *Ignited Minds*, President Kalam calls knowledge the prime mover of prosperity and power. For him, knowledge is associated with education but also with the skills of artists, craftsmen, philosophers, saints, and homemakers. In his view, academic learning coexists with the earthy wisdom of villages and the hidden knowledge of the environment.[3] These broad visions of content and audience are shared among participants in the Million Book Project.

In the Million Book Project, we adopted two collection strategies: one around best books, using *Books for College Libraries*, and another around agricultural content. Each of these was inspired by copyright implications. The question of selection arises repeatedly in an attempt to assure that in some large scanning project the best books are being identified and brought to the web. The identification and use of lists to select books for digitization adds greatly to the cost of any project. If the vision/assumption is that all books will be scanned, it would appear to be a waste of money to generate such lists and try to work from them. However, as more and more monographic content comes to the web, the pressure to identify the better or best items will again arise and will be resolved, as discussed next, in new ways.

The Universal Library directors are interested in the scientific and societal benefits of scanning books and other formats. To the extent that agreement can be reached with our international partners, we are willing to share our content under non-exclusive agreements. We have been surprised by the political difficulties in getting participants to share content, inasmuch as digital copying is easy and the original still remains at its first location. Nevertheless, some of our content already resides in the Open Content Alliance site. We hope that access to all content can eventually be facilitated for all world audiences.

Google Book Search

There are limits to what an outsider can know about Google Book Search, and further limits about what an insider is allowed to discuss. Nonetheless, it is clear from "News and Views" history, talks by Google staff, and discrete accounts from some library partners that Google, the Million Book Project, and OCA share a vision of distributing of useful knowledge to the world, despite having widely different means, processes, and underlying goals. Since Google is the focus of this collection of essays, other authors will no doubt elaborate from their perspectives.

Google Book Search's driving philosophy is "To organize the world's information and make it useful and web-accessible." In a *Wall Street Journal* article, Google CEO Eric Schmidt wondered, "How many users will find and then buy books they never could have discovered any other way? How many out-of-print and backlist titles will find new and renewed sales life? How many future authors will make a living through their words solely because the Internet has made it so much easier for a scattered audience to find them?"[4] These ruminations offer a powerful antidote to the worries of publishers and a very few other copyright holders worldwide and are discussed more fully in the third section of this article.

Open Content Alliance

Brewster Kahle, the innovator behind the Internet Archive, is the creator of the Open Content Alliance (OCA), a group of cultural and technological organizations that will build a permanent archive of multilingual digitized text and multimedia content. This content will be accessible soon through the OCA website and through Yahoo! Over thirty libraries and cultural organizations are a part of the OCA and plan to share their digital collections in this manner.

Kahle has a proprietary scanner and offers to scan materials onsite at a cost of about ten cents a page, but the project also accepts materials that have been scanned using member libraries' own equipment and techniques. The OCA website records that 100,000 books had been loaded onto its servers by December 20, 2006. The website also notes that the University of Illinois at Urbana-Champaign is making its newly dig-itized collection of Abraham Lincoln books accessible through OCA. The University of Pittsburgh Library System has just started a project to digitize its Darlington Memorial Library, a rich resource in early Amer-ican history. That project will add some 11,000 volumes, 3,000 photo-graphs, and hundreds of maps to OCA.

AUTHORITY IN SCHOLARLY WORK

In his *New York Times* article, "Scan this Book," Kevin Kelly con-cludes that books want to be freely accessible on the web and that the barriers, fierce though they may be, will be overcome by the pressures of customer demand. Kelly notes, "The desire of all creators is for their works to find their way into all minds."[5] He believes there is a moral imperative to scan, and notes that Amazon is busily scanning the four million books in its inventory.[6]

Many librarians remember that there was a time of scarcity before the advent of the web. A librarian's task was to help students find–through intricate sets of print indexes–materials that might be appropriate for their work. In "The New Metrics of Scholarly Authority," Michael Jensen equates this specialized knowledge of available resources to the shamanic authority in a prehistoric hunter-gatherer tribe. The shaman knew the best places to find food for the tribe.[7] By contrast, Google and its kin provide a time of information abundance; the experts in such a society are those who can select and prepare it best. To continue the food analogy, authority now accrues to the chef whose skills are para-mount.[8] A new breed of librarians who are "more progressive and hip-per" are cooking up great things for clients.[9]

Jensen, the director of strategic web communications for the National Academies, writes that old measures of authority will be replaced by new ones. In the paper environment, authority was conferred through number of citations, quality of journals, and institutional affiliation of the author. As society moves through Web 2.0, authority models are changing to ones in which popularity and applause confer prestige. Google page rank allows one page to vote for another and designate some pages as more important than others. Similarly, librarians them-selves are conferring prestige on sites by referencing them from web guides created for students. Social networking sites and group-participa-tion engines are playing a role in client selections of materials to use.[10]

Jensen argues that a long list of markers will be used to confer reputation and authority. These new markers will be:

- Prestige of the publisher
- Prestige of peer pre-reviewers
- Prestige of commentators
- Percentage of document quoted
- Raw links to document
- Valued links
- Discussion in blogs, etc.
- Nature (positive, negative, interconnective . . .) of language
- Quality of the context
- Percentage of phrases valued by a disciplinary community
- Quality of author's institution
- Significance of author's other works
- Author's participation as commenter, editor, etc.
- Reference network
- Age of document
- Inclusion in best lists
- Type of authoritative tags[11]

Clearly, some sophisticated weighted algorithm will be used to collect these metrics and present them as some type of ranking.

Existing ranking lists, such as the *U.S. News* ranking of universities, and the Association of Research Libraries list, do confer authority. Many institutions discuss them in the context of a sophisticated understanding of the components of the ranking, and of the ways in which resources can be applied at the institution level to manipulate placement. One university librarian noted that her efforts to clear out a longstanding cataloging backlog had the unintended but pleasant consequence of creating a jump in the ARL rankings. Another university official observed that the ARL algorithm was sensitive to the number of librarians and could be manipulated by adding professional staff. Clever computer algorithms and programs will be subject to some manipulation by even cleverer individuals.

For two or three years, using Rory Litwin's article "On Google's Monetization of Libraries"[12] as a construct, I gave an interactive talk in various U.S. and international venues about the Million Book Project and Google Print. Litwin obsesses about the prospect of having machines do some of the reading and indexing for humans. He thinks that software solutions can never achieve the kind of precision provided by catalogs and indexes interpreted by reference librarians. Nevertheless, information seekers do find the simplicity of a single search box compelling, and librarians must work with computer scientists to make these new tools as proficient as possible. Some librarians in the audience were anxious about this prospect, but the computer scientists in the audience were eager to talk about evolving mechanisms. Jensen's thoughts on the new metrics of scholarly authority do rely on much broader approaches than closed peer review and editorial authority. If machines can do much of the preparation for librarians, then we can serve our clients an even more delightful dish.

Jensen predicts the replacement of the old metrics of authority with the new within ten to fifteen years. He notes that scholarly output locked away on hard drives, in print only, and behind firewalls will be invisible to the web crawlers and indexers. He concludes, "Scholarly invisibility is rarely the path to scholarly authority."[13] For the scholarly journal, that is a resounding endorsement of open access journals and self-archiving of individual content. For the monograph, he says "it's past time that scholarly publishers started talking seriously about new models, whatever they turn out to be–instead of putting their heads in the sand and fighting copyright-infringement battles of yesteryear."[14]

National Academies Press experimented in 1998 by putting the full text of its new books online and found that sales of print volumes increased.[15] In 2006, Rice University began an A. W. Mellon-funded project to produce online scholarly monographs. These projects suggest that alternatives are available. Kelly's remark about the author's desires is powerful in the scholarly community where authors' reputations– rather than publishers' profits–are paramount.

COPYRIGHT:
THE BIGGEST BARRIER

The largest barrier to the success of large digitization projects as they attempt to attain their visions for a better, more equitable and productive world is copyright. A recent OCLC study of the books in the original five libraries of the Google Print project (now called Google Book Search) discovered that only about 20 percent of the 10.5 million unique titles in this collection are out of copyright–if books published before 1923 are assumed to be out of copyright. In contrast, out-of-copyright books are the stated primary objective of the Million Book and OCA digitization projects.

While there are many, many details in the international agreements about copyright, the World Intellectual Property Organization signatories are generally bound by the same time parameters. This section discusses several alternative efforts to overcome this barrier: Non-renewed books, Digital Library Federation (DLF) next steps for non-renewed books, permission work, government publications, a new Chinese law, and synthetic documents.

Non-Renewed Books

In the United States, books were initially granted copyright for fourteen years, after which that copyright could be renewed for fourteen more years. Over the next two centuries, the duration of copyright was extended repeatedly. The Copyright Act of 1976 eliminated the requirements of copyright registration and renewal for new works and extended the renewal term for earlier works. The result is that the copyright status of works published between 1923 and 1963 depends on whether the copyright was renewed. Research conducted by the Copyright Office in 1960 revealed that less than 15 percent of all registered copyrights were renewed, and that the renewal rate for books was only seven percent.[16] More recently, informal studies, conducted by Dr. Michael Lesk[17] and others, indicate that 80 to 90 percent of the books published during this period were not renewed.

In the Million Book Project, we were able to select materials for scanning from the Carnegie Mellon University Libraries collection by doing a machine comparison of a date range of titles in our collection with the copyright renewal records. Dr. Lesk used scripts to do the comparison and to generate a list of books that did not appear to have had their copyright renewed. These books were then shipped to China for scanning and were returned. Of course, as these books appear on the web, publishers and authors may identify works for which copyright was renewed and notify the project. Those books will be removed from the digital collection immediately. Denise Troll Covey has described this work in her monograph *Acquiring Copyright Permission to Digitize and Provide Open Access to Books*.[18]

Digital Library Federation:
Next Steps

At the April 2007 Digital library Federation (DLF) Forum, Dr. John Ockerbloom of the University of Pennsylvania Libraries convened a meeting on copyright issues. The participants agreed that the most important breakthrough in overcoming the copyright barrier could be achieved by creating a list of U.S. books published between 1923 and 1963. The bibliographic records for these books could be compared with the copyright renewal records. The result would be a list that could be labeled, with the help of intellectual property attorneys, in such a way that scanning operations would be able to scan the books and bring them to the web. With any such list, the scanning project would have to be willing to remove a work if notified by the copyright holder that copyright had been renewed.

OCLC's Bill Carney[19] was at the 2007 DLF Forum. He indicated that OCLC is thinking through the issues attendant to aggregating evidence of copyright status for titles represented in the WorldCat bibliographic database. Librarians connected with the Google Book Search project, the Million Book Project, and other digitization projects are now helping to define functional requirements for a copyright evidence registry service, and preparing to contribute locally created sources of copyright status data.

Permission Work

As the Million Book Project developed, our collection strategy was to identify the best books that could be included in the project. Librarians associated with the project turned to the venerable *Books for College Libraries* as a source of highly desirable content. Ms. Troll Covey had the insight that, rather than seek copyright permission title by title, we should identify the publishers whose work was most often represented and ask them for permission to digitize some or all of their out-of-print titles. Troll Covey provides detailed metrics in her book: basically, about 20 percent of scholarly and association publishers agreed to have some of their out-of-print materials included in the Million Book Project.[20]

Agreements with these publishers dictated an approach to display and printing because the publishers wanted individuals to be able to print only one page at a time so that readers would be encouraged to purchase books rather than printing them out. Publishers also wanted copies of the digital files so that they could mount them on their own web sites, hoping to achieve the increased interest that the National Academies Press reported.

Government Publications

Copyright concerns drove another collection initiative inside the Million Book Project. The United Nations' Food and Agriculture Organization was interested in having its content digitized, and that led to exploration of a partnership with the National Agriculture Library. Academic libraries with agriculture collections were interested in having some scanning done in China. Those materials, many of which are government publications of counties, states, and the U.S. Department of Agriculture, either are not copyrighted or are copyrighted with agencies who can give permission for digitization. In 2006, a shipment of agriculture collection materials was sent to the scanning center in Shenzhen, China.

In 2005, U.S. Public Printer Bruce R. James visited the Universal Library directors with a team from the Government Printing Office to learn about how they might implement the assigned task of bringing all the content created by the GPO to the web. Subsequently, GPO began a large, distributed digitization project whose results are available at <http://www.gpoaccess.gov>.

A New Chinese Law Regarding Copyright

At the annual Million Book Project conference in 2006 at the Biblioteca Alexandrina, the provost of Peking University described a new Chinese law that allows scholarly books published in China to be scanned while under copyright. These books then can be made available online to students at the over 800 universities and colleges in China. This extraordinary development allows the Chinese to share new intellectual content among students and faculty immediately and effectively. China's ambitions to excel in science and technology education and achievement are well served by this strategic legislation.

Synthetic Document Alternative

At the 1st International Conference on the Universal Digital Library in Hangzhou, China, Dr. Michael Shamos, one of the directors of the Universal Library Project, talked about creating synthetic documents in a talk entitled "Machines as Readers: A Solution to the Copyright Problem." Dr. Shamos, who has a Juris Doctor degree, as well as a doctorate in Computer Science, finds that the existing copyright treaties, compulsory licensing, and public lending rights agreements fall short of the needs of visions for bringing academic content to the web. He says, "[M]aking use of the international consensus that copyright does not protect facts, information or processes, we propose to scan works digitally to extract their intellectual content, and then generate by machine synthetic works that capture this content, and then translate the generated works automatically into multiple languages and distribute them free of copyright restrictions."[21] This exciting idea would allow many, many works to have their content used to advance learning, especially in the fields of science and technology, around the world.

While novels, poetry, and a whole host of other types of works will not allow for synthetic document creation, works in technical fields are well suited to this treatment. Creating a pilot project to test this idea is a high priority for Carnegie Mellon, where our Language Technologies Institute is focused on translation and summarization issues and where our University Counsel has a strong interest in intellectual property issues.

CONCLUSIONS

When I obsess about how journal price increases and the general dysfunction in the scholarly communication system are killing libraries, my colleague Michael Shamos reminds me of how quickly and thoroughly the hand-held calculator replaced the slide rule. Major digitization projects are making huge headway toward bringing scholarly content to the web. Many challenges exist in the process of transforming to a new construct for scholarly authority and to new roles for librarians in a time of information abundance. Copyright issues must be a key focus for all engaged in these projects in order to bring more high quality content to the web. The vision of equitable, worldwide access to the accumulated knowledge in monographs is being achieved on a number of fronts, particularly now that Google has joined the effort as a major player.

NOTES

1. Google Book Search number by e-mail from Ben Bunnell, Manager of Library Partnerships for Google Book Search (August 7, 2007).

2. Second International Conference on Universal Digital Library (ICUDL): <https://www.bibalex.org/icudl06/>.

3. Kalam, A. P. J. Abdul. *Ignited Minds: Unleashing the Power Within India* (New York: Viking, 2002), 121-127.

4. Schmidt, Eric. "Books of Revelation." The *Wall Street Journal* (October 18, 2005). <http://googleblog.blogspot.com/2005/10/point-of-google-print.html> [August 31, 2007].

5. Kelly, Kevin. "Scan this Book!" *New York Times Magazine* (May 14, 2006). <http://www.nytimes.com/2006/05/14/magazine/14publishing.html?ex=1305259200en= c07443d368771bb8ei=5090> [August 31, 2007].

6. Ibid.

7. Jensen, Michael. "The New Metrics of Scholarly Authority." *The Chronicle of Higher Education; The Chronicle Review* (June 15, 2007). <http://chronicle.com/free/ v53/i41/41b00601.htm> [August 31, 2007].

8. Ibid.

9. Jesella, Kara. "A Hipper Crowd of Shushers," *New York Times* (July 8, 2007). <http://www.nytimes.com/2007/07/08/fashion/08librarian.html?ex=1200974400&en= 8cb7403e5f48a28c&ei=5087&excamp=mktat5> [August 31, 2007].

10. Jensen.

11. Ibid.

12. Litwin, Rory. "On Google's Monetization of Libraries." *Library Juice*, 7, 26 (December 17, 2004). <http://libr.org/juice/issues/vol7/LJ_7.26.html#3> [August 31, 2007].

13. Jensen.

14. Ibid.

15. Pope, Barbara Kline. How to Succeed in Online Markets: National Academy Press; A Case Study. *Journal of Electronic Publishing* 4, 4 (May 1999) <http://www. press.umich.edu/jep/04-04/pope.html> [August 31, 2007].

16. Ringer, Barbara A. "Renewal of Copyright" (1960 study). Reprinted in *Copyright Law Revision; Studies Prepared for the Subcommittee on Patents, Trademarks and Copyrights of the Committee on the Judiciary* (Washington: U.S.G.P.O., 1961), 220.

17. Dr. Michael Lesk is on the faculty of the Library and Information Science department, SCILS (School of Communication, Information, and Library Studies), Rutgers University.

18. Troll Covey, Denise. *Acquiring Copyright Permission to Digitize and Provide Open Access to Books* (Digital Library Federation, 2005).

19. Bill Carney is Product Manager in the Business Development Division at the Online Computer Library Center (OCLC).

20. Troll Covey.

21. Shamos, Michael I. "Machines as Readers: A Solution to the Copyright Problem." *Journal of the Zhejiang University SCIENCE Special Proceedings Issue of the First International Conference on Universal Digital Library* (ICUDL, 2005), 1179. <http://www.zju.edu.cn/jzus/2005/A0511/A051102.pdf> [August 31, 2007].

Using Metadata to Discover the Buried Treasure in Google Book Search

Millie Jackson

A recent article in *The Economist* estimated that 10 million books per year are being scanned around the world through Google Book library partnerships.[1] Over the past year I have experimented with Google Book Search in my own research and in my position as a collection development librarian. The advantages as well as the disadvantages for researchers and for librarians have become apparent. Millions of books available at the click of the mouse is certainly an advantage; however, several questions regarding metadata come to mind. How does the metadata that Google supplies enhance research and assist researchers in locating what they need? What can the library contribute from the bibliographic record and its metadata?

Through the library partnerships Google has access to decades of collection development work by some of the top ranked libraries around the world to build its online presence in Google Book Search. The power of Google Book Search truly becomes apparent when we consider what this provides for users: the ability to easily discover rare texts as well as texts with small runs, the potential for providing wider access to information once only available by physically visiting a library, the potential to discover unknown authors' and works. While many have found fault with Google Book Search and Google's corporate secrecy, the transformation of the way we work as scholars and researchers is tremendous.

In this article I will explore what I have discovered about the metadata Google captures as well as comparing it to the MBooks project at The University of Michigan. MBooks, unveiled in August 2006, draws the data Google has scanned from The University of Michigan Libraries into its online catalog to promote further access to the digital copies of texts. I will also compare metadata in Google Book Search with metadata in WorldCat, using it as a representation of our online catalogs.

METADATA

What does metadata do? Simply put, it makes items accessible and discoverable. Good metadata allows the user to locate an item easily and in an organized way. Metadata moves beyond the basics of description, becoming a part of the object itself in a digital project like Google Book Search. Examining the metadata provided with Google Book Search records along side metadata in a bibliographic record, one can see pros and cons for both. One can also see where one may inform the other. Google Book Search draws on several types of metadata to bring together a variety of resources that are related to a work.

Metadata in Google Book Search is retrieved from a number of sources according to Ben Bunnel of Google.[2] These sources provide a richer record than the brief catalog record; however, they are not without problem. Some of the metadata is automatically harvested which creates some interesting results. The question is, do those results hinder the experience or not?

Libraries have been attempting to do the same thing–draw resources together in one place for easier searching. Rather than find fault with what Google Book Search is doing, we should be looking for ideas. The resources which appear at the bottom of the page are not always those a librarian or faculty member would point out but they allow opportunities for discussing critical thinking and evaluation skills. They may also reveal resources that we would not find or which would take more time to find.

NAME AUTHORITY

One of the early problems encountered when searching Google Book Search is that one can not retrieve everything that had been scanned and included in Google Book Search by a particular author. I initially thought that this was a problem of name authority–names were not normalized but rather, they are scanned and entered as they appear on the title page of a book.

My experimentation involved locating works by fairly obscure 19th-century women writers. As I searched for books by Mrs. A. D. T. Whitney I discovered that I had to search for a number of variants on her name in order to locate all the works included in Google Book Search.

This discovery was a delight and a frustration as I marveled over how much easier some of my research could have been if Google Book Search had been available a decade ago. I initially questioned how I would have known that the books were under Mrs. Whitney's full name, initials, or partial initials but as I have thought about this and the research process I realized that I had to hunt through a wide variety of indexes and abstracts for this information, some from the 19th century, to locate all of her works. The information was not all easily accessible as I spent a few years hunting down many of the authors and their works in various libraries around the country and tried to borrow books to read with mixed success. This is all part of a graduate student's or a faculty member's research process and puzzle.

Since I could not find all of the results in one search, I submitted a question to Google about name authority. Shortly after this, I attempted my search again and I could find all of Mrs. Whitney's works in one search. Whether it was my question or the constant evolution of Google Book Search that caused the improved search is not clear.

Saul Hansell described how Google is "constantly tweaking the company's search engine in an elusive quest to close the gap between often and always."[3] Hansell's article details the way in which the engineers behind Google's search engine pay attention to failed searches and strive to provide searchers with what they want. Amit Singhal is quoted as saying "Search over the past few years has moved from 'Give me what

I typed' to 'Give me what I want.' "[4] This creates great expectations for users not only of Google, but also of all resources on the Internet.

KEYWORDS AND PHRASES

Out-of-copyright works in Google Book Search provide a string of keywords and phrases at the top of the record. These words are one of the things that initially caught my cataloger's eye. They made little sense when compared to subject headings provided in bibliographic records. However, conversations with people at Google reveal that the metadata provided here is based on frequency of the word's appearance in the text. The advantage, of course, is that the searcher can search an entire work whether those key words and phrases make sense or not.

My question is whether or not the keywords and phrases really add anything to the Google Book Search record? In my searches for *The History of Miss Betsy Thoughtless* by Eliza Haywood, I primarily found examples of character names. In other examples I found less useful words due to the frequency with which they occur in the text. The string of keywords does not really add much value to my research. I can click on a name and locate a list of references in the text but I can also do that by using the "search this book" feature and have the words highlighted in the context where they appear.

I compared the Google Book Search keywords to what I found in WorldCat under subject headings. While both can be retrieved on either the title or the author's name, the Google Book Search record misses what catalogers sometimes refer to as "aboutness" that is captured in subjects. Subject headings included terms such as "married women" and "abused wives" as well as geographic and chronological headings. If a searcher begins with broad topics, then a search in WorldCat may produce a different set of results. Depending on the keywords it may or may not be narrower than the same search in Google Book Search. To get at the same kind of "aboutness" in Google Book Search would take further manipulation of the search because the searcher accessing the full text rather than the subject of a work. There are pros and cons to both kinds of searches. Either one may yield surprises and provide results for texts the searcher did not expect to discover. Clicking on a subject heading may take the searcher to like works that would be more relevant or would widen a search for material on a given topic. The keywords and phrases in Google Book Search provide little assistance in this regard, since these words are connected directly to the text at hand and provide a list of where the word or phrase appears in the work.

The power of Google Book Search and its keyword functions lie in what it will allow the user to access–full text of millions of books, in copyright, out of copyright, in print and out of print. The "searchin this book" feature is also included on each record's page so researchers may use their own keywords to search within the book. This is where, despite the metadata that does not meet traditional bibliographic standards, we can discover works which may assist with research and collection building. Searches can be constructed for words, phrases, or subjects within the books available, whether in copyright or out of copyright, to discover if the work will be useful. This is a distinct advantage.

Other features are more useful in Google Book Search, however. For works that are in copyright, a blurb about the book appears at the top of the record and the keywords and phrases drop to the bottom. This feature provides far more than a list of keywords or a list of subject headings. It offers the searcher an overview that tells him or her far more about the work and allows him or her the opportunity to decide if it is exactly what is wanted.

CONCEPTS

Concepts are often no easier to locate in the online environment than they were in the print environment. Still, concepts can be more easily located in full text archives than they can in searching for subject headings or by conducting keyword searches in an online catalog. For example, when searching for the concept of "pin money," a term for women's spending money commonly used in the 18th century, in Google Book Search I was able to narrow the search quickly to texts that were relevant. Since the term is highlighted in the text, one can quickly determine the context and if this will be a useful document for research. I was able to find the exact term in Google Book Search since it allows full text searching whereas I could only locate instances of the two words, or one of the words, in my search of WorldCat. WorldCat is not, of course, full text but since "pin money" is not a subject heading I could not as easily determine if there were articles in *The Spectator* or where they were as I could in Google Book Search.

WorldCat reveals articles from some databases, which is a useful feature. But in the second entry "pin" appears in a formatted content note

so this book, though not relevant to my search, appeared high in the results list. Further refining by looking at subject headings in the results
would have produced a better list of works but one would still have to
search for the full text or for a print copy.

NEEDS FOR RESEARCHERS:
THE RARE ITEM

Google Book Search can be valuable for the esoteric research some
faculty undertake and can assist with ILL requests which sometimes can
not be filled because of the age or rarity of a work. A faculty member
came to us with a request for a rare article on oysters published in the
19th century. While Google Book Search was not our first stop in searching for this request, it was the source that provided the full text. We initially searched the usual sources looking for a copy of the article for the
faculty member. I then turned to Google Book Search, not expecting to
find a journal article but did, in fact, find a reprint in a monographic series. I did not find the exact citation but I found the article in another
source because of the ability to search full text. The search required some
fine-tuned keyword searching and the use of the advanced search screen
in Google Book Search.

The faculty member had the full text in PDF format at his finger tips.
We were able to fulfill a request easily and inexpensively which we might
not have been able to fulfill at all otherwise.

While this is one anecdote about the potential for using Google Book
Search, it demonstrates the usefulness of the growing number of full text
archives that we often forget exist. Google Book Search is by no means
the only free resource we have available to promote to people but how
often do we remember that resources like Making of America, Victorian
Women Writers, or even Project Gutenberg may provide the full-text
resource that a user needs to answer a question or complete a paper?

Robert B. Townsend noted some of his concerns in an article dated
April 29, 2007 in *AHA Today*.[5] Townsend worries about some of the
scanning errors he has found in Google Book Search as well as a lack of
OCR. While I have not seen scanning errors corrected recently, on July
2, 2007 Google began making OCR available on its site. The scanning
errors include pages scanned twice or blurred scans. Townsend also notes
the poor metadata that I have already noted.

We should remember that Google Book Search, like many Google projects, is still in Beta. Despite the millions of texts now freely available, it is still testing and tweaking information. This is not said to dismiss errors; but rather to note that changes and improvements are inevitable.

MBOOKS

One question that has come up at conferences and in articles is how libraries will incorporate Google Book Search into existing services. Should libraries catalog the Google Books? Should they include Google Books in their catalogs or as a link on Websites?

In August 2006 The University of Michigan, one of the original library partners, announced MBooks as part of its answer for integrating the Google Book Search project into its online catalog, Mirlyn <http://mirlyn.lib.umich.edu>. The project has already been subjected to usability tests and the books that are not restricted by copyright are freely available to those who want to search Mirlyn. What are the pros and cons of this project for someone outside the Michigan community?

Michigan has been one of many universities engaged in creating digital projects with partners for the past 10-20 years. Information about the MBooks project can easily be found on the library homepage <http://mdp.lib.umi ch.edu>. I will not discuss the technical aspects of the project but want to focus on research. Currently the library is incorporating links for books in the public domain, works that are uncopyrightable, and works for which Michigan has permission from the copyright holder. If a work is still in copyright, then a message will appear letting the searcher know he or she can search the full text but not view it. This becomes somewhat tricky in the digital age both for the library doing the scanning and for the researcher trying to find a digital copy that he or she can access. For example, The University of Michigan's copy of *The History of Miss Betsy Thoughtless* is not available through MBooks because it is also included in Gale's Eighteenth Century Collections Online (ECCO). This may be due to licensing or copyright restrictions and agreements.

Obviously the faculty and students at The University of Michigan are the main audience for searching within Mirlyn, but there are also advantages for those outside the Michigan community. According to Suzanne Chapman, Interface and User Testing Specialist at The University of Michigan, there is currently not a way to limit a search to only MBooks or to identify an MBooks title in a search list.[6] Several upgrades are in the planning stages, however. Chapman stated that one of the advantages of Michigan's implementation is the option for a full text view in OCR. (As noted above, this is now also available in Google Book Search.) This is beneficial for students using screen readers and can be used by anyone, not just those affiliated with The University of Michigan. Michigan's implementation demonstrates how libraries can draw together print and electronic resources developed by partnerships and make them discoverable to anyone who has access to the Internet. Searching in Mirlyn presents different options for viewing texts than Google does and also presents the option to identify where the copy of the print book is held if the researcher wants to borrow it. There are advantages in both systems and watching the way they develop, as well as what other library partners do with their data, will be fascinating.

In MBooks it is more important to know exactly what you are searching for than it is in Google Book Search. This represents, in part, the difference between searching a full text source and an ILS.

Michigan's version has some advantages for how the researcher is able to read a work online. There are more options and the screen layout is different than that in Google Book Search. The page turner feature allows people to simulate reading a book online as they would in print.

The choice between Google Book Search and an implementation like The University of Michigan's may come down to personal preference. Each implementation includes rich features, with the promise of more as the projects develop.

The research process changes on the Internet. The expectations are that it should be easier but that is not necessarily true, no matter what online source we are using. Google Book Search does present a tool which can potentially be a great help in that process, however, and draws librarians into the equation by drawing on their search skills and knowledge of collections. Since the Google records also provide a link to "find the book in a library" this provides further opportunities for discovery and for leading researchers back to the library and discovering works that may not be immediately apparent if only using Google Book Search. This link takes the searcher outside of Google to WorldCat and searches across multiple union catalogs, showing the closest library to the user's location. If, as planned, OCLC includes records with links to Google Book in WorldCat, this makes the library even more important as a source for discovering not only electronic works but also related print resources.

In May 2007, Lorcan Dempsey wrote in his blog "We sometimes talk about Google as if it is something fixed: we know what it does and how it works. . . . We do not know what Google will be like three years time–it will certainly not be the Google of today."[7] The one thing we know for certain is that Google will continue to tweak and change its interface. What will libraries do to integrate Google into their interface or to build upon what they learn and observe from Google?

NOTES

1. "Not Bound By Anything," *The Economist*, March 22, 2007 [accessed May 19, 2007].

2. I spoke to Ben Bunnell and Jennifer Parsons at ALA Annual in Washington, D.C. on June 23, 2007.

3. Hansell, Saul. "Inside Google's Black Box." *New York Times*, June 3, 2007, national edition.

4. Hansell.

5. Townsend, Robert B. "Google Books: What's Not to Like?" *AHA Today*, April 29, 2007. <http://blog.historian.org> [accessed May 27, 2007].

6. E-mail correspondence with Suzanne Chapman, May 21, 2007.

7. Dempsey, Lorcan. "Universal search and the rich texture of suggestion," Lorcan Dempsey's weblog. May 18, 2007.

Google Video–
Just Another Video Sharing Site?

Tine Walczyk

Video sharing has been a practice for as long as the Internet has been pervasive in our culture. Prior to 2005, when users wanted to share videos, they were mainly traded through ftp sites or individuals' websites. Some companies put their videos on CDs or DVDs and mailed them to customers. Although video files were plentiful, they did not reside in publicly accessible repositories. There was no cohesive way to retrieve them. Each storage location had a different interface and was step-intensive. As a result, no means of cross-referencing existed.

In the era of Reality TV, amateur videos have become a significant portion of Internet traffic. Web 2.0 has come to the world of video. Now, there are sites that specifically allow anyone to upload any video and have it be available to the public, without having to manage their own film catalog. These servers and services function as sharing communities. Anyone with the ability to record a video–be it from their cell phone or in a production studio–can have an audience in minutes. All of these sites allow for search capability and cross-referencing. Most follow the Web 2.0 paradigm of allowing the Internet community at large to be responsible for its content, organization, and regulation. Some extend to allow for community building features such as channels, sharing, tagging, and "friend"-ing.

Since then, the technology has been harnessed to allow for several variances in implementation. Other sites, for example, IFILM and AOL Video, focus on sharing professional-grade videos with options to buy or sell. Generally, they are much more standardized in their organization, policies, and appearance. However, even these sites are beginning to employ some limited use of "participatory media" (Deuze 2006, 63) as a value-add to draw in customers. So, whether it's the professional media with a movie trailer or Joe Crumb from Iowa wanting to show off his 20-pound fish, video sharing appears to be here to stay.

A highly unscientific survey of technology geeks in Austin, TX revealed the following most common video sharing sites: YouTube.com, Google Video (video.google.com), iFilm.com, Broadcaster.com, AOL Video (video.aol.com), and Uncut Video (uncutvideo.aol.com). I had heard of YouTube, but the rest had been unknown to me. Very little was found in my literature search, but I have included information on what I was able to find. This article reports on usability testing on each site and provides an unbiased explanation and comparison of their features.

GOOGLE

Google technically has two players in the video sharing arena: Google Video and YouTube. As a search tool, Google blazed the way in simultaneously searching for videos with other types of Internet content. However, as a provider of video content, "Google (search) delivers results only from its own YouTube and Google Video–along with third party MetaCafe" (Louderback 2007, 7). To Google's credit, when

YouTube was purchased, it retained a healthy dose of independence and the two products were not combined into one. This allows it to be available to all. Each tool has its unique qualities and is listed separately below.

GOOGLE VIDEO

Google Video focused originally on providing online access to video already in existence from the mainstream media. It allows the categorization, searching, and purchasing of these videos. One of the strongest features of this tool is its basis in the Google search engine. The advanced search options and the ability to set search preferences make it stand out from other sites.

Recently, it has added the ability for users to upload their own content. This content is moderated (reviewed) for copyright issues amongst others and released within several hours. The user gets to define several options upon uploading the video including whether it is free or not, whether it is publicly available, title, and description. A major strength of Google Video over its competitors is its lack of size and run-time restrictions. This allows for distribution of everything from a complete lecture or board meeting to a performance or wedding video (Sweetow, 2007). A minor detraction is that the only access points available to the video are a choice of three genres, which limits the searchers' ability to find their video.

YOUTUBE

YouTube first appeared on the scene in 2005 to provide a solution to video sharing, searching, and browsing. It had a wide range of unintended effects. YouTube opened the door for end users to have an "audience of millions for free" (Karim 2006). In October 2006, Jawed Karim, one of the co-founders, noted that it served 100 million videos a day, had 30 million visitors per month, and was responsible for 58% of all of the videos shown on the Internet. YouTube allows for unrestricted content to be placed on the Internet. It does not actively review uploaded items and only removes items at the copyright owner's request.

According to its website, YouTube is a way to get your videos to the people who matter to you. With YouTube you can:

- Uplgraoad, tag, and share your videos worldwide
- Browse thousands of original videos uploaded by community members
- Find, join, and create video groups to connect with people with similar interests
- Customize your experience with play lists and subscriptions
- Intete YouTube with your website using video embeds or APIs (YouTube 2007).

All of these features bring to light the main difference between this product and others. They exhibit the concept of "participatory media," which falls in the Social Networking category that Web 2.0 boasts. YouTube has developed into a place where anyone with the ability to use a video recording device, be it cell phone, digital recorder, or webcam, can distribute that clip to a world wide audience.

IFILM

According to its website, IFILM is a leading online video network, serving user-uploaded and professional content to over ten million viewers monthly. IFILM's extensive library includes movie clips, music videos, short films, TV clips, video game trailers, action sports, and its popular "viral videos" collection. IFILM is one of the leading streaming media networks on the Internet (Gillmor, 2004).

IFILM has positioned itself as a leader in distribution of mainstream media online. In conjunction with Viacom (its parent company), it provides copyrighted material from within the collection of companies. Also, now part of the MTV family (a subsidiary of Viacom), "iFilm [*sic*] also has an extensive legit music-video area. The interface is slicker and better organized than YouTube's, and video quality is superb" (Samiuan, 2006). On top of this, when YouTube made its debut, IFILM stuck its toes into the participatory media. It was the wild success of amateur video that caused IFILM to open an area on its site for users to upload their own videos.

AOL

Like Google, AOL has two players in the online video sharing market: AOL Video–used to find traditional and for-pay items–and Uncut Video–where users can upload their own creations. "What sets AOL (Video) apart from its competition is the breadth and scope of its other channels. It is here that AOL video proves it isn't some fly-by-night startup, but a company with the backing of a media giant (Time Warner)" (Holahan, 2006). AOL Video's search engine is designed to pull from both tools and somewhat uniquely from other video sharing sites as well. The main hurdle for users is that AOL Video incorporates advertising throughout its offerings, even integrating them into the video clips themselves. Although AOL Video stands up to the quality and quantity of offerings that IFILM boasts, Uncut Video lacks some of the powerful features of Google Video.

BROADCASTER

Broadcaster incorporates the participatory philosophy of the other tools, but takes media to the next level of true social networking. Users can upload and share their videos and become instant producers, but they can also become live media outlets. Broadcaster allows for live webcams, video e-mail, music, and a rich set of communities. Finally, it provides software tools to help users create, edit, and upload their videos. Its professional presentation along with dedication to the user makes this site one definitely useful for more than storage.

Table 1 summarizes the features of the sites reviewed in this article.

CONCLUSION

My first impressions as a librarian drew me to the more "professional" looking, highly categorized sites such as iFilm and AOL Video. In fact, it took me a while to see the appeal of Google Video and YouTube at all. Today, however, even I can see the need for both. I have learned to put aside my bias for blatant order and the packaging and become willing to join the populist spirit associated with Web 2.0.

TABLE 1. Summary of Site Features

	Google Video	YouTube	IFilm	AOL Video	Uncut Video	Broadcaster.com
Moderated	Yes	No	Yes	N/A	Yes	No
Participatory Media	Yes, a little	Yes, completely	Yes, a little	No	Yes	Yes, even includes options for live interactive webcasts
Free or Pay Per View	Both	Free	Both	Both	Free	Both
Simple Search Tool	Yes	Yes	Yes	Yes	Yes	Yes
Advanced Search Options	Yes	No	No	No	No	No
Refining Search Options	No	Yes	No	No	No	No
Stickiness of Search Results	No	Yes	No	No	No	No
Limiting Categories	Yes	Yes	Yes	No	No	Yes
Explanation of Copyright policy	Yes–hidden one layer underneath terms of service statement Also found in Help	Yes–appropriate named link at bottom of page	Yes–hidden in terms of use statement	N/A	Yes–hidden in video license agreement, very short	Yes–hidden in terms and conditions statement
Login Required to Upload	Yes (Processing is done after your upload. Not real-time)	Yes	Yes	N/A	Yes	Yes
File Types Accepted	AVI, MPEG, Quicktime, Real, and Windows Media	.WMV, .AVI, .MOV, and .MPG	XVID, DAT, 3GP, ASF, AVI, DV, GVI, FLV, MOV, MP4, MPEG, MPG, QT, or WMV	N/A	.3gp, .3gp2, .avi, .dv, .mpg, .mpg4, .mov, .mqv, .wmv	Not specified
Available Through RSS	Yes	No	Yes	Yes	No	No

REFERENCES

Deuze, Mark. 2006. "Participation, Remediation, Bricolage: Considering Principal Components of a Digital Culture." *Information Society*, 22 (2): 63-75.

Gillmor, Dan. 2004. *We the media: Grassroots journalism by the people, for the people*. Sebastopol, O'Reilly Media Inc. <http://www.oreilly.com/catalog/wemedia/book/index.csp>.

Holahan, Catherine. "AOL Video: Close But No TiVo." *Business Week Online*, August 7, 2006: 7.

Karim, Jawed. 2006. *YouTube: From Concept to Hyper-growth*. <http://www.youtube.com/watch?v=nssfmTo7SZg>. (Accessed August 1, 2007).

Louderback, Jim. 2007. "Google's Gambit." *PC Magazine*, July 17: 7.

Samiuan, Tom. 2006. "Beyond YouTube." *Rolling Stone*, 1007: 35.

Sweetow, Stu 2007. "You Tube GENERATION: Creating Viral Videos Via User-Generated Content Sites." *EventDV*, 20 (7): 28-34.

YouTube. What is YouTube? YouTube Help Center. <http://www.google.com/support/youtube/bin/answer.py?answer=55749&ctx=sibling>. (Accessed June 21, 2007).

Google's Bid to Build Cooperation and Partnerships Through Librarian Central and Google for Educators

Robert J. Lackie

INTRODUCTION: FOCUS AND INTENT

Google has continued to crank out new Web-based products at an astounding rate, even if some of the fun Google Labs' past and current projects have not sparked much interest in the library or teacher communities. As a professor and an education librarian, I am happy to hear that there is now an initiative to care about products or services done in collaboration with or of immediate value to librarians and teachers. Two promising initiatives that came out of librarian and teacher conversations with Google offer some proof that it is beginning to listen to us: the Google Librarian Central and Google for Educators sites. This article will briefly look at the background of these two initiatives and related projects, such as The Literacy Project, by the search and advertising giant, and how libraries, schools, and others view their value and impact.

REACHING OUT TO LIBRARIANS

After talking with and surveying many librarians for about a year, Google decided that what librarians really wanted was an online site where we could easily interact with each other and learn more about the potential uses of cool Google tools and services. In late December 2005, Google launched the Google Librarian Center, now called Librarian Central, to that end. As Tom Peters pointed out in his article, the e-mail newsletter on the site was specifically geared toward librarians and "as a newsletter *can* signify an attempt to court or woo someone, this one, aimed at librarians, apparently grew out of the feedback Google received at their booth" (2006, 7) at the 2005 ALA Conference in Chicago. Google representatives were certainly present at many forums and presentations at the 2005 Internet Librarian Conference in Monterey, as well, greeting librarians and handing out "Google loves librarians" cards with a note about signing up for the soon-to-be released online newsletter. Whether or not we all agreed with the first sentence on the new site, "Librarians and Google share a mission to organize the world's information and make it universally accessible and useful," the second sentence stated that "The goal of this newsletter is to highlight ways we can work together to fulfill that mission for patrons, students and users"–and it seems that we all could appreciate the "working together" aspect.

According to Patricia Steele, Dean of University Libraries at Indiana University Bloomington, that quote on the Web site "marks a major shift in the information landscape–from one where libraries and librarians 'owned' this mission to one where commercial competitors provide viable and even affordable alternatives to traditional libraries of all kinds" (2006, 6). Steele points out that a conclusion of the OCLC study, *Perceptions of Libraries and Information Resources* (De Rosa 2005), is that libraries of all types have begun to lose their position as "the primary and first access point for information."

Although libraries continue to be a place where information and Internet access are freely available, Steele states that "all library staff must understand their role in bringing users to the library–physically and virtually. . . . When we are not the only game in town, we have to be the most attractive, comfortable, and easiest to use" (2006, 7). I would like to think that all librarians would basically agree with this premise, but I also think that this should not hinder us from working together with Google, Yahoo!, the Internet Archive, or any other organization that might be able to help us better serve our users. That being said, what is the Google Librarian Central doing for us as librarians and educators?

Since the December 2005 launch of the Librarian Center Newsletter, Google continued to release quarterly updates, providing news and reviews, as well as input from end users like us. Past issues (Google Librarian Central Newsletter Archive 2007) have included interviews with Google engineers and developers, and from the very first newsletter, Google has invited us as librarians and library supporters to send our thoughts, opinions, and questions about Google, as well as "stories of how librarians use and keep up with technology on the job," promising to "do [their] best to use [our] feedback to make each issue more relevant and useful to the library community" (Healy 2005). Initially, this forum was not very interactive since our responses to Google were limited to e-mail only.

Fortunately, as the owner of Blogger, Google realized, after listening to our requests, that a better tool for this communication would be a blog, and in January 2007, the Librarian Central blog was born, and the March 2007 issue included the best blog posts from the Librarian Central blog. The Librarian Central blog is now far more interactive than the original Librarian Center site, although it does not allow anonymous comments, and comment moderation has been enabled, requiring that all comments be approved by the blog author. Content is posted more often (usually weekly) and readers can subscribe to it via Gmail, the personalized Google homepage, or another blog reader or RSS feed.

The main page now includes a "Teaching Tools" link to posters and online activities to help patrons and students get the most out of using Google tools and services. There are also short videos and articles of other librarians showing how they are using Google in creative ways. In addition, you can view the newsletter archive, determine which librarian conferences Google representatives will be attending in order to chat with them, and read a list of library blogs Google recommends.

Although there is always room for improvement, the one general complaint that I have seen in the blogosphere about Library Central, besides Google waiting too long to enable their comments for the blog, was that the stories, librarian quiz, and examples/tips are too North American-centric, heavily biased toward United States searchers. As one English blogger asks, "Why does Google consistently ignore librarians who are not based in North America? If they don't have the time or resources available to create different resources then the very least they could do would be to make the ones they do have a little more global in appeal" (Bradley 2007)–I guess that is something for Google to work on, and I am sure they will accept suggestions on this. Still, the blog/newsletter to include the diversity of the content, have come a long way in a year or so. I recommend signing up for the newsletter or getting the RSS feed and checking the site out for yourself–and then contribute to it.

CONTINUING IN BID TO BUILD COOPERATION AND PARTNERSHIPS

While Librarian Central was demonstrating the beginnings of success in consolidating the newest information for librarians into a new and improved go-to site, Google was making some promotional waves in other areas, and October 2006 proved to be a busy month for Google in their bid to garner new partnerships and improve their outreach efforts. For instance, it was in October that Google announced that they had joined with the Frankfurt Book Fair, the United Nations Education, Scientific and Cultural Organization's (UNESCO's) Institute for Lifelong Learning, and other literacy and educational organizations to form the long-term literacy project called Frankfurt Book Fair Literacy Campaign (LitCam 2007) to help combat illiteracy around the world. The Fair used the activities and public events to draw international attention to the plague of functional illiteracy around the globe, including illiteracy in industrialized nations, and it plans to continue the event, with the next one taking place on October 9, 2007. One of the goals was to develop joint projects or campaigns, bringing more participation from other organizations.

What Google did during the Fair to assist with goals was to announce its launch of a literacy search site called The Literacy Project (2007), a "resource for teachers, literacy organizations and anyone interested in reading and education, created in collaboration with LitCam, Google, and UNESCO's Institute for Lifelong Learning." This new site is criticized by some as being nothing more than a promotional stunt in the context of a humanitarian mission, only highlighting the use of Google tools, such as Google Maps, which is currently being used on the site to geographically locate literacy efforts, and Blogger is promoted as a free way to share ideas and communicate among interested parties. I have to admit that I would like to see Google do more with this new site, as since its inception, I have not seen that it offers anything more than it did in late 2006. However, I must also say that Google did not have to do anything to assist with LitCam, and although I am sure this brings more attention to other Google products on the site (Google Book Search, Google Scholar, Google Video, Google Groups, and Google Co-op), these are freely available and practical products and services. I do hope the site becomes more useful and helps achieve LitCam's objectives. At this point, however, very little is being said about The Literacy Project, unlike another project and its related services launched a week later, Google for Educators.

REACHING OUT TO EDUCATORS

As I noted earlier, October 2006 was a busy month for launching projects for Google. Similar to the Librarian Central and The Literacy Project sites, this new Google for Educators site consolidates into one location a number of Google tools, this time tools aimed at K-12 educators. There has been quite a bit of talk and many comparisons made about this site.

According to *Education Week*, the Google for Educators site, announced on October 11, 2006, came about because of a response to educators' requests for information and assistance in using and teaching with Google tools. "Google started developing Google for Educators after getting an increasing number of e-mails from teachers asking for help, said Cristin Frodella, the company's product-marketing manager for K-12 education. Many wanted to know how best to teach students to use Google's popular search engine, she said" (Borja 2006, 9). Originally, the site began by providing basic information and teachers' guides for 12 Google products: Google Web Search, Earth, Book Search, Maps, Video, Docs and Spreadsheets, Blogger, SketchUp, Calendar, Picasa, Google Apps for Your Domain, and Google Personalized Homepage. Additionally, a few examples and lessons of how teachers in the United States were using these tools were provided and highlighted:

> A teacher in Virginia uses Picasa with his students to create picture collages of famous Americans. At a school in California, teachers use Google Calendar to schedule events and reserve resources such as the computer lab and projectors. One teacher in Chicago has her students practice graphing data using Google Earth, the spreadsheets in Google Docs & Spreadsheets, and earthquake data from the U.S. Geological Survey. And students across the country completing their English homework on the word processor in Goo-

gle Docs & Spreadsheets will always be able to find that assignment, no matter what computer they're working on. (Google Press Center 2006)

With this education initiative, it is clear that Google has begun a campaign for teachers, throwing its hat in the educational arena. Add this to the announcement from Matt Katzive at Discovery Education that Google was collaborating with it "to create online lessons and digital videos to supplement Google Earth" (Borja 2006, 9), as well as noting that Google had brokered a "deal with U.S.-based virtual learning application provider Blackboard to help Google develop search technology for education" (Smith 2006, 2), and now no one can argue that Google is not aiming for teachers.

Immediately after the launch of Google for Educators, notices, comments, and opinions varied. At the PBS Teachers blog, one blogger wrote concerning this new teacher site that "the collection is somewhat shallow in its [October 2006] current form. For example, the information provided about their popular Blogger.com service is pretty thin on the ground, containing just a few promotional paragraphs. . . . And unfortunately the 11 other products promoted on the site don't have much more meat to them either. So far, the initiative hasn't exactly started a firestorm of discussion in the educational blogosphere, but a handful of educators are talking about it." The post continued later by stating that "Google for Educators seems more like a promotional stunt, lacking in any new resources tailored for educators" similar to The Literacy Project (Carvin 2006).

Some looked at the initiative a bit differently, though Roddy MacLeod, Senior Subject Librarian at Heriot-Watt University in Riccarton, Edinburgh believes that having Google "interested in these areas creates competition for other service providers and keeps them on their feet. Librarians need to accept this. We can't keep our heads in the sand" (Smith 2006, 2). And Paul Harrington, Business Analyst Manager for the Serco Group in London, "which helps schools offer e-learning, said it is a smart move by Google. 'It's a huge market, and it's only going to grow with the government's current policies' " (ibid). And Julie Lindsay, Educational Technology Specialist at International School Dhaka, Bangladesh, was "most impressed with the user-friendly tutorials and ideas linked to each tool" at the new site, although she was wondering if and when Google would "broaden this to include international educators," referring to the site and the in-person teacher education development sessions scheduled to be provided only in California at the time (Lindsay 2006).

I would have liked to have seen a little more primary source material, more interesting ideas, articles, and tutorials showing how these Google tools could be used in creative and valuable ways, but it was only a beginning attempt. I think many people were looking for the site to immediately provide details of how to really use these Google tools in significant ways so that teachers could immediately implement them more easily in the classroom. I understand that thinking, because it was what I expected as well, with Google being such a Web 2.0 powerhouse, and it certainly was what I was hearing in my teacher workshops. Still, like the Google Librarian Central established before it, this site will probably need some time to become more developed and useful. As one Ed-Tech Insider blogger put it when the Google for Educators site was first established, "Google is taking a small first step, where it will go is hard to say. . . . However, on the whole, I'll take a company that puts out lots of useful applications at no cost over one that is good at networking but bad at writing code" (Hoffman 2006), suggesting that Google could still improve its communication and outreach efforts.

Many teachers I spoke with suggested that Google hire more teachers to help it with outreach efforts to educators. I am not sure how much Google will follow that advice, but there certainly was some buzz about offering the first Google Teacher Academy on November 7, 2006 with a prominent declaration on the Google for Educators site. This Academy was touted as a free, intensive, one-day professional development opportunity at their headquarters, for K-12 educators to gain "hands-on experience with Google's free products and other technologies, learn about innovative instructional strategies, receive resources to share with colleagues, and immerse themselves in an innovative corporate environment. Upon completion, Academy participants become Google Certified Teachers who share what they learn with other K-12 educators in their local region" (Google Teacher Academy 2007).

This was certainly one way to get valuable teacher input, and I applaud their thinking, even if at this time, they have not yet offered any webinars, instead still only providing the one-day in-person sessions for "K-12 educators within a 90-minute local commute of an Academy event." Fortunately for interested teachers, Google has expanded locations since providing the first Academy at its Mountain View, CA headquarters, offering the second event on February 15, 2007 in New York City, and the third on May 23, 2007 in Santa Monica, which, by the way, included librarians from Orange, Simi Valley, and Long Beach,

CA. It plans on offering more in-person sessions, but I have not heard anything official about plans to open up an online Academy as of yet, although the Google for Educators representative Cristin Frodella was quoted as stating that her "company hopes to offer more seminars for teachers, both in person and on the Web" (Borja 2006, 9) in 2007–I will be looking forward to that.

In addition to the "Tools for your classroom" link to basic information and teachers' guides for Google products and the "Google Teacher Academy" already discussed above, other prominent links on the current June 2006 Google for Educators site include the Infinite Thinking Machine blog, and under the "Teacher Community" link, the new Google for Educators Discussion Group started in March 2007, in addition to a place to enter your e-mail address to sign up for the Teacher Newsletter.

On the "Tools for your classroom" page, the link for one of the original 12 Google products, Google Video, has interestingly been removed, perhaps because many schools block many video search sites. Also, three recent additions to the "Tools" page are Google Groups, Google News, and Google Page Creator, with the "Personalized homepage" name changed to the new iGoogle. Like the Librarian Central site, links to posters to help get the most out of Google products are provided, and a few more "real-world examples of innovative ways that teachers and librarians are using Google tools to help students learn" have been added to the original "Classroom activities" page. With a promise from Google that many more examples will be added, my guess is that these will probably come from the Google Teacher Academy graduates, known as Google Certified Teachers.

One great example of a project being developed by Google Certified Teacher Jerome Burg from Granada High School in California is his Google Lit Trip site, which takes a literature piece students are studying, such as *Macbeth*, and plots out the characters' travels using Google Earth. Jerome has examples for grades K-5, 6-8, 9-12, and higher education faculty (Burg 2007). Steve Hargadon, an Open Source guru and educator, provides a good description of this site, as well as an audio link to Burg's project, over at the Infinite Thinking Machine (ITM) blog (Hargadon 2007).

Speaking of the ITM blog–my favorite Google-sponsored blog for teachers–I believe this is one of the best links on the Google for Educators site. Backed by Discovery Educator Network and WestEd, among others, ITM's goal is to show how technology can impact student learning, and the posts are very interesting. Because the posts are written mainly by educators, they are very relevant and useful to teachers and instruction librarians, leading us to other educational articles and innovators. I mentioned the post above from Hargadon as an example, and another contributor to the blog, Wesley Fryer, Director of Education Advocacy (PK-20) for AT&T in Oklahoma, has recently presented a session about Google for Educators and "the wealth of powerful free tools" (Fryer 2007a) that are found there for learners.

Fryer's PBwiki site for his recent presentation, "Using Google Tools for Educational Research and Collaboration," brings together some of his favorite Google teaching resources, ideas, articles, tutorials, and other materials. His presentation was about how Google tools "permit streamlined Internet research, connecting ideas, hyperlinks and data with geographic places on earth, collaboratively authoring documents with options to share the results with others, creating web pages with a web browser, and more" (Fryer 2007a). Other educators, like eighth-grade teacher Marilyn Steneken, are using some of the Google tools, like Sketch-Up, to enhance a class project Create-a-Culture wiki, where students use the Google 3-D drafting tool in "constructing the homes and buildings associated with their culture" (Higgins 2007a). I am sure that more educators like Fryer and Steneken, and more Google Certified Teachers like Burg, will be providing additional innovative ways that teachers and librarians can help students learn, with the Google tools assisting. More of these real-world uses may be shared on the main Google for Educators and Google Librarian Central sites, as well as through their newsletters, blogs, and discussion groups.

Although I find the ITM blog to be my favorite networking/learning tool on the Google for Educators site, Google encourages teacher networking via the new Google for Educators Discussion Group (2007) that I mentioned earlier, initiated in March 2007. Currently, the membership in that group is less than 900 and the activity a bit low, even with all of the press that the site is being given. The group is meant to be a "discussion forum where you can exchange information with other teachers–information about using Google, as well as other innovative learning techniques & tools in the classroom," and according to the site, anybody can join or view group content. The topics are presently centered around the use of Google tools in the classroom, education resources (like using Blogger Widgets to distribute educational content), current events, lesson planning, and the Google Apps Education.

Although there is not a lot in the discussion group or in articles about the Google Apps Education, there are some interesting articles and comments on the Web. Certainly, as Higgings points out at his high school (2007b), more and more teachers are learning about and using the Google tools, and according to *Education Week*, Google Apps is

> used by schools as well as colleges and universities, includes Customizable Web pages, instant-messaging tools, e-mail, and interactive calendars. Tens of thousands of educational institutions and organizations, including the 65,000 students at Arizona State University in Tempe, use Google Apps, said Kevin Gough, a product-marketing manager for the company. (Borja 2006, 9)

Google Apps Education Edition (2007), according to Google, is a "broad IT solution that schools can use to bring communication and collaboration tools to the entire academic community for free. Google manages all the technology details, so you can focus your time, energy and budgets on teaching your kids." It combines, or you can mix and match, the following services for your school: Gmail (the chat function can be disabled for the school), Google Talk, Google Calendar, Google Docs and Spreadsheets, and Google Page Creator. So why would some schools not go for this?

PC World Canada states that "Google Apps provides great free or cheap applications, but implementing these in your home or your network can also come with a price . . . and may bring tough consequences" (Rickwood 2007). Besides Arizona State University mentioned earlier, Lakewood University in Ontario is also an example of a large user of Google Apps, with its "more than 38,000 users recently migrated to the Education Edition, and they now have Gmail and in-browser IM capabilities as a result." However, the Lakewood University Faculty Association did not agree with the use of Gmail as their e-mail service provider, filing a grievance with the University because "as many observers have noted, working with the Google service can expose individual users, and their communications and their data."

That sounds ominous. It was, however, the published comment from Rob Harmer in response to and located at the end of the *PC World Canada* article mentioned above that really caught my attention. Harmer states that "the key issue to be faced is the one relating to Intellectual Property [IP] protection. With Google Apps you have NO RIGHTS to the content (your IP) once posted via the apps for collaboration on the Web" (Rickwood 2007). He goes on to link to a feature article by anti-piracy and management advice business PCProfile.com, entitled "Managing 'Google Tools' to reduce risk," which states that organizations must have acceptable use policies in place before using the free Google collaborative tools. Additionally, it urges that we all should understand that according to Google's Terms and Conditions of Service, "by submitting, posting or displaying Content on or through Google services which are intended to be available to the members of the public, you grant Google the . . . right to syndicate Content submitted, posted or displayed by you on or through Google services and use that Content in connection with any service offered by Google" (PCProfile 2007). This may be a major reason why the faculty at Lakewood University object to the Gmail service. Clearly Google does not guarantee privacy or IP protection, so I would not recommend uploading sensitive (personal or university) documents over the Web via the free Google tools.

CONCLUSION:
THE VALUE AND IMPACT
OF THESE INITIATIVES

Yes, Google continues to astound us–and make some nervous–with its numerous free Web-based products and services. And now, it has sparked interest in the library and teacher communities with the promising initiatives and projects related to the Google Librarian Central and Google for Educators sites. This article has provided background and opinions from librarians, school teachers, and others on what Google has done for librarians and teachers lately and I encourage you to explore these special, targeted Google projects, services, and tools aimed at librarians and other educators. I am sure there will be more articles and posts on the value and impact on many of Google's endeavors, especially the Librarian Central and Educators sites, and possibly even The Literacy Center.

If they find the tools discussed here useful, perhaps fewer educational institutions will decide to block and ban Google use. Unfortunately, I continually hear more about school districts around our country blocking the entire Google Web site, not just a particular Google tool, such as Google Video or Blogger. I have been amazed at how many teachers in New York and New Jersey have recently been telling me that they have no access to any Google tools, not just Blogger, at their schools.

Wesley Fryer mentioned the same thing when he heard that school districts in Oklahoma and Texas block the entire Google domain. He does understand how elementary or even middle schools might want their students to use more age-appropriate tools, but blocking Google at high schools, too? "I think high school students should definitely have access to Google for searches at school. And students at all levels should have access to other powerful Google tools." He later states that "working online without Google is analogous to someone trying to swim without using their arms and just kicking their feet" (Fryer 2007b).

I understood Fryer's comment and am sure Google very much appreciated it. I am also sure that Fryer would agree with PCProfile's sentiments that users, to include all students, should be better educated in the use of Google tools, especially regarding the privacy and security of sensitive content, and that users/students should develop the ability to discern advertising and inappropriate resources on the Web from useful and scholarly materials.

Whatever your opinion of Google and its motives, you will find Librarian Central to be a worthwhile site, consolidating the newest information into easily digestible formats and providing a networking opportunity for librarians of all types–it has improved immensely this past year. As for The Literacy Project and the Google for Educators sites, they do attempt to place Google in context with larger goals of humanitarian and educational organizations, which is OK with me. Sure, Google is out to make a profit–we know this–and Google certainly needs to address particular issues with its services and tools, but I like the fact that it is taking some time to talk to us and build sites that allow for the sharing of software/technology that most of us individually and even collectively within our organizations might not be able to afford, as well as making them easily available to us and our students from home.

Google is, without a doubt, very good at promoting itself and bringing issues of concern to the forefront, even unexpectedly, but it does seem that when Google does place its feet in a certain arena, others seem to follow suit–has anyone looked at the newest Yahoo! Teachers (2007) site? It just makes you love search engine competition! Maybe with our assistance, the search giants can develop a decent student-safe search engine/directory that would not be blocked at schools.

REFERENCES

Borja, Rhea R. 2006. Google for Educators unveils interactive tools for schools. *Education Week*, November 29, 9.

Bradley, Phil. 2007. Google Librarian Central: Talking at librarians. Search Engine Land blog, January 19. <http://searchengineland.com/070119-054527.php> (accessed May 30, 2007).

Burg, Jerome. 2007. Google Lit Trips. <http://www.googlelittrips.org> (accessed June 5, 2007).

Carvin, Andy. 2006. What's up with Google for teachers? Learning.now blog, October 13. <http://www.pbs.org/teachers/learning.now/2006/10/whats_up_with_google_for_teach.html> (accessed May 30, 2007).

De Rosa, C. 2005. *Perceptions of libraries and information resources: A report to the OCLC membership.* Dublin, OH: OCLC.

Fryer, Wesley. 2007a. Using Google tools for educational research and collaboration. Teach Digital: Curriculum by Wesley Fryer wiki. <http://teachdigital.pbwiki.com/googletools> (accessed June 2, 2007).

Fryer, Wesley. 2007b. School without Google? Techlearning blog, February 23. <http://www.techlearning.com/blog/2007/02/school_without_google.php> (accessed June 4, 2007).

Google Apps Education Edition. 2007. <http://www.google.com/educators/p_apps.html> (accessed June 6, 2007).

Google for Educators. 2007. <http://www.google.com/educators> (accessed June 6, 2007).

Google for Educators Discussion Group. 2007. <http://www.google.com/educators/community.html> (accessed June 6, 2007).

Google Librarian Central. 2007. <http://librariancentral.blogspot.com> (accessed June 3, 2007).

Google Librarian Central Newsletter Archive. 2007. <http://www.google.com/librariancenter/librarian_newsletter.html> (accessed May 28, 2007).

Google Press Center. 2006. K-12 educators put new Google resource center to the test. <http://www.google.com/press/annc/educators.html> (accessed May 29, 2007).

Google Teacher Academy. 2007. <http://www.google.com/educators/gta.html> (accessed June 6, 2007).

Hargadon, Steve. 2007. A great "mashup": Mapping literary journeys. Infinite Thinking Machine blog, March 13. <http://www.infinitethinking.org/2007/03/great-mashup-mapping-literary-journeys.html> (accessed June 5, 2007).

Healy, Jodi. 2005. Welcome to the first edition of the Google Librarian Newsletter. Google Librarian Newsletter, December. <http://www.google.com/librariancenter/newsletter/0512.html> (accessed May 24, 2007).

Higgins, Patrick. 2007a. STEP students using Google SketchUp. Tech Dossier blog, February 23. <http://techdossier.blogspot.com/2007/03/power-of-google.html> (accessed June 2, 2007).

Higgins, Patrick. 2007b. The power of Google. Tech Dossier blog, March 9. <http://techdossier.blogspot.com/2007/02/step-students-using-google-sketchup.html> (accessed June 2, 2007).

Hoffman, Tom. 2006. Google Apps in schools. Ed-Tech Insider blog, October 16. <http://www.eschoolnews.com/eti/2006/10/001573.php> (accessed June 4, 2007).

Lindsay, Julie. 2006. Google-centric learning. E-Learning Blog, October 13. <http://123elearning.blogspot.com/2006/10/google-centric-learning.html> (accessed June 2, 2007).

LitCam, Frankfurt Book Fair. 2007. <http://www.litcam.org/litcam/en/index.php> (accessed June 4, 2007).

The Literacy Project. 2007. <http://www.google.com/literacy> (accessed June 7, 2007).

PCProfile. 2007. Is your IP leaking - 2: Office collaboration. <http:// www.pcprofile.com/Office_Collaboration.pdf> (accessed May 30, 2007).

Peters, Tom. 2006. Google corner(ed): And finally . . . Google's Newsletter for Librarians. *Young Adult Library Services* 4(3): 7.

Rickwood, Lee. 2007. *PC World Canada*, March 23. <http://www.pcworld.ca/Pages/NewsColumn.aspx?id=8088b6470a01040800f483b40707b39a> (accessed June 6, 2007).

Smith, Laura. 2006. Google aims at educators. *Information World Review*, November, 2.

Steele, Patricia A. 2006. Blurring the lines: Academic and public libraries revisited. *Indiana Libraries: The Journal of the Indiana Library Federation and the Indiana State Library* 25(3): 6-8.

Yahoo! Teachers. 2007. <http://teachers.yahoo.com/home> (accessed June 7, 2007).

Index

Page numbers followed by *n* refer to notes; those in **bold** refer to tables; those in *italics* refer to figures

Printed and bound by CPI Group (UK) Ltd, Croydon, CR0 4YY

01/11/2024

01782628-0001